Learn Portuguese

A Guide to Learning the Basics of a New Language

By Jenna Swan

© Copyright 2015 by Jenna Swan - All rights reserved.

In no way is it legal to reproduce, duplicate, or transmit any part of this document in either electronic means or in printed format. Recording of this publication is strictly prohibited and any storage of this document is not allowed unless with written permission from the publisher. All rights reserved.

The information provided herein is stated to be truthful and consistent, in that any liability, in terms of inattention or otherwise, by any usage or abuse of any policies, processes, or directions contained within is the solitary and utter responsibility of the recipient reader. Under no circumstances will any legal responsibility or blame be held against the publisher for any reparation, damages, or monetary loss due to the information herein, either directly or indirectly.
Respective author own all copyrights not held by the publisher.

Legal Notice:
This book is copyright protected. This is only for personal use. You cannot amend, distribute, sell, use, quote or paraphrase any part of the content within this book without the consent of the author or copyright owner. Legal action will be pursued if this is breached.

Disclaimer Notice:
Please note the information contained within this document is for educational and entertainment purposes only. Every attempt has been made to provide accurate, up to date and reliable complete information. No warranties of any kind are expressed or implied. Readers acknowledge that the author is not engaging in the rendering of legal, financial, medical or professional advice.
By reading this document, the reader agrees that under no circumstances are we responsible for any losses, direct or indirect, which are incurred as a result of the use of information contained within this document, including, but not limited to, - errors, omissions, or inaccuracies.

Table of Contents

Chapter 1: The Portuguese Alphabet

Chapter 2: Pronunciation Guide

Chapter 3: Greetings and Basic Phrases

Chapter 4: Numbers

Chapter 5: Months, Days, and Seasons

Chapter 6: Telling Time, Date, and Year

Chapter 7: Weather and Seasons

Chapter 8: Colors in Portuguese

Chapter 9: Introductions

Chapter 10: Family

Chapter 11: Describing People

Chapter 12: Asking for Directions

Chapter 13: Getting Around

Chapter 14: Finding a Place to Stay

Chapter 15: Ordering Food in a Restaurant

Chapter 16: Shopping

Chapter 17: Forming Portuguese Sentences

Chapter 18: Nouns and Articles

Chapter 19: Pronouns

Chapter 20: Adjectives

Chapter 21: Verbs

Chapter 22: Adverbs

Chapter 23: Prepositions

Chapter 24: Vocabulary

Chapter 1: Portuguese Alphabet

Portuguese evolved from ancient Latin, one of the five modern romance languages along with Spanish, Italian, French, and Romanian. It developed in Portugal but Portuguese explorers brought the language to South America and other parts of the world. Today, it is spoken by more people in Brazil, which is the home country of about 90% of Portuguese speakers. While it is not a distinct language, the development of Brazilian Portuguese was greatly influenced by its own culture and history. Hence, there are notable differences between the Portuguese spoken in Europe and Brazil in terms of spelling, pronunciation, grammar and vocabulary.

The 1990 orthographic agreement among Portuguese-speaking countries aimed to eliminate discrepancies in spelling among the many variants of the language. The agreement was made mandatory at the start of 2015 after several years of transition and had the following effects:

- the inclusion of the letters "k", "w", and "y" in the official Portuguese alphabet
- the elimination of diaeresis marks and acute accent
- the removal of the letters "c" and "p" from spelling whenever these letters are silent
- the establishment of guidelines on capitalization and hyphenation

In addition, the agreement considers the remaining differences in spelling as legitimate.

Here is the Portuguese alphabet as used in Brazil and Portugal:

Letters	Letter Names	
	Brazilian Portuguese	European Portuguese
Aa	á	á
Bb	bê	bê
Cc	cê	cê
Dd	dê	dê
Ee	é or ê	é
Ff	efe	efe
Gg	gê	gê or guê
Hh	agá	agá

Ii	i	i
Jj	jota	jota
Kk	cá	capa
Ll	éle	éle
Mm	eme	eme
Nn	ene	ene
Oo	ó or ô	ó
Pp	pê	pê
Qq	quê	quê
Rr	erre	erre or rê
Ss	esse	esse
Tt	tê	tê
Uu	u	u
Vv	vê	vê
Ww	dáblio or duplo vê	dâblio or duplo vê
Xx	xis	xis
Yy	ípsilon	ípsilon or i grego
Zz	zê	zê

Chapter 2: Pronunciation Guide

The phonetic system of Portuguese is quite extensive. Its most distinguishing feature is nasalization in many sounds which is indicated by the use of tilde. Portuguese also uses the grave, acute, and circumflex accents in its vowels and the cedilla in letter c.

Vowels	Example	English sound
a, á, stressed	aluno (student)	like "a" in father
ã	não (no)	nasal sound, like the "an" in angry
ê	você (you)	like "ey" in they
é, stressed	café (coffee)	like "e" in let
e, unstressed	leite (milk)	like "a" in make
i	camisa (shirt)	like "ee" in see
o, unstressed	livro (book)	like "oo" in book
ô	avô (grandfather)	like "ow" in know
ó, stressed	avó (grandmother)	like "aw" in law
u	uva (grape)	like "oo" in too

Common Diphthongs	Example	English sound
ão	dão (they give)	nasalized, like "own" in town
au	causa (cause)	like "ou" in house
ei	meio (half)	like "ay" in day
eu	Europa (Europe)	like "you"
ia	tia (aunt)	ee-ah, like "ee" in meet+"a" in far
ie	dieta (diet)	like "e" in yet
io	rio (river)	ee-oh, like "ew" in new
oi	oito (eight)	like "oy" in toy
ua	suar (to sweat)	like "wa" in water

Consonants	Example	English sound
b	bala (candy)	like "b" in bag
c before a, o, u	coro (choir)	hard like "k"in kit
c before e and i	cedo (early)	soft like "c"in city
ç before a, o, u	aço (steel)	soft like "c"in city
d	data (date)	like "d" in door

g before e and i	dia (day)	like "j" in jungle
f	faca (knife)	like "f" in four
g before a, o, u	gato (cat)	hard like "g" in gate
g before e and i	gelo (ice)	soft like "s" in pleasure
gu before a, o, u	água (water)	hard like "gw" in Nicaragua
gu before e and i	guia (guide)	soft like "gu" in guide
h		silent
j	jornal (newspaper)	like "s" in treasure
k		used for borrowed words
l		like "l" in leave
l after a or i	Brasil (Brazil)	like "w" in few
m	mapa (map)	like "m" in money
m as the final letter	bom (good)	halfway between "m" and "n"
n	nada (nothing)	like "n" in neat
n after a vowel	conta (bill)	like "n" in contract
p	pato (duck)	like "p" in part
q	aqui (here)	like "k" in kite
qu before a, o, u	quando (when)	hard like "kw" in quick
qu before e and i	que (what)	like "k" in key
r start of a word	rico (rich)	hard like the "h" in heat
r between 2 vowels	caro (expensive)	like "tt" in butter or "dd" in ladder
r after a consonant	branco (white)	like "tt" in butter or "dd" in ladder
rr	marrom (brown)	hard "h" like in "heat"
s	sopa (soup)	like "s" in song
s between vowels	casa (house)	like "z" in zoo
s in unstressed -es	estar (to be)	like "as" in taste
t	tomate (tomato)	like "t" in trap
t before e and i	arte (art)	like "ch" in cheese
v	você (you)	sounds like "v" in victory
w		for borrowed words
x initial letter	xícara (cup)	like "sh" in she
x before a vowel	próximo (next)	like "s" in song
x between vowel	táxi (taxi)	like "x" in tax
x after e	exato (exact)	like "ays" in ways
y		for borrowed words
z	luzes (lights)	like "z" in zoo
z end of a word	luz (light)	like "s" in song

Common Digraphs	Example	English sound
ch	cheque (check)	like "ch" in machine
lh	trabalho (work)	like "ll" in million
nh	amanhã (tomorrow)	like "ni" in onion
sc	piscina (swimming pool)	like "s" in song
sç	desça (go down)	like "s" in song
ss	osso (bone)	like "s" in song

Chapter 3: Greetings and Basic Phrases

Greetings, courtesy words, and survival phrases are essential aspects of learning a new language. Here are the most common Portuguese phrases with their pronunciation:

Olá!	O-lá	Hello!
Oi!	oi	Hi! (informal)
Bom dia!	bon DEE-ah	Good day!
Boa tarde!	boh-AH TAR-dee	Good afternoon!
Boa noite!	bo-AH NOI-chee	Good evening!
Como está?	KOH-moh ish-TAH?	How are you?
E aí? (colloquial)	Oy? ee ah-ee	So, what's up?
Bem/muito bem.	Baing/moo-ee-toh baing	Well/Very well.
Tudo Bem.	TOO-do BENG	Everything is fine.
Bem, obrigado/a.	BENG, ob-ree-GAH-doo/dah	Fine, thank you
Muito mal.	moo-ee-toh mao	Very bad.
Mais ou menos.	Ma-eece oh meh-nos	More or less, so-so
De nada.	je NAH-dah	You're welcome.
Obrigado. (male speaker)	ob-ree-GAH-doo	Thank you.
Obrigada. (female speaker)	ob-ree-GAH-dah	Thank you.
Como vai?	Coh-moh vye?"	How's it going?
Como está?	KOH-moh ish-TAH?	How are you?
Sim.	SEEN (Brazil)/SEE (Port)	Yes.
Não.	NOWNG	No.
Perdão.	pehr-DAWNG	I'm sorry.
Desculpe.	desh-KUL-pay(Brazil)/desh-KULP (EP)	I'm sorry.
Com licença!	co-lee-sensah	Excuse me.
Não faz mal!	nah-fash-mahl	No problem.
Está bem!	tah baing	It's okay.
Por favor.	pohr fa-VOHR	Please.
Até mais!	ah-tay myee-sh	See you soon.
Até logo.	ah-TEH LOH-goo	See you later.
Tchau!	CHOW	Goodbye! (informal)
Adeus!	uh-DEOOSH	Goodbye!
Você fala Inglês?	fah-lah ing-GLEZH?	Do you speak English?
Não falo Português.	NOWNG fah-loo por-too-GEZH	I don't speak Portuguese.
Socorro!	soo-KOO-hoo!	Help!

Compreendo.	kohn-pree-EHN-doh	I understand.
Não sei!	naw say	I don't know.
Não compreendo.	NOWNG kom-pre-EN-doo	I don't understand it.
Não entendi!	naw en-tehn-chee	I didn't understand it.
Não entendo!	naw en-tehn-doo	I don't understand it.
Pode repetir?	pod ray-peh-teer?	Could you repeat, please?
Onde é a banheiro?	OND-de eh a bah-NYAY-row?	Where is the toilet?

Best wishes

Feliz aniversário!	Happy birthday!
Parabéns!	Congratulations!
Feliz Ano Novo!	Happy New Year!
Feliz Natal!	Merry Christmas!
Saúde!	Cheers!
Feliz Páscoa!	Happy Easter!
Boa sorte!	Good luck!
Boa viagem!	Have a nice trip!
Boa sorte!	Good luck!
Boas férias!	Have a nice holiday!
Bom apetite!	Enjoy your meal!
Bom divertimento!	Enjoy yourself/Have fun!
Bom fim de semana!	Have a nice weekend!

Chapter 4: Numbers

Cardinal Numbers

Numbering guidelines

Portuguese units and tens digits from zero to nineteen are specific words that should be memorized. Numbers sixteen to nineteen are derived by combining the tens and units digits.

Likewise, the tens have specific names. Except for numbers 10 and 20, the rest of the tens digits are derived from the root of the ones digits. Thus, sixty is "sessenta" from the unit digit "seis" and seventy is "setenta" from the unit digit "sete".

You use the same rules for the hundreds digits. The number 100 is "cem" and its plural is "centos". Thus, two hundred is "duzentos" (dois + centos) and four hundred is "quatrocentos" (quatro + centos).

An "e" which means "and" is used to link tens and units digits. For example, the number 22 is "vinte e dois" (twenty and two). An "e" is also used to link thousands and hundreds ending in two zeroes (mil e trezentos, 1,300). Thousands and unit digits are likewise connected by an "e" (dois mil e três, 2003).

In Portuguese, like in most European languages, a period is used to separate the thousands from the hundreds digits and the thousands from the millions digits. When a number has decimal digits, a comma is used instead of the period.

Example:

English   4,255,136.22
Portuguese 4.255.136,22

The Cardinal numbers:

0	zero	zeh-ro
1	um	oohm
2	dois	doy-z
3	três	tray-eess
4	quatro	kwa-troh
5	cinco	seen-koh
6	seis	say-z

7	sete	seh-chee
8	oito	oy-too
9	nove	noh-vee
10	dez	deh-z
11	onze	ohn-zee
12	doze	doh-zee
13	treze	treh-zee
14	quatorze	kwah-tour-zee
15	quinze	keen-zee
16	dezesseis	deh-z-ee-say-z
17	dezessete	deh-z-ee-she-chee
18	dezoito	deh-z-oy-too
19	dezenove	deh-z-ee-noh-vee
20	vinte	veen-chee
21	vinte e um	veen-chee e oohm
22	vinte e dois	veen-chee e doy-z
30	trinta	treen-tah
31	trinta e um	treen-tah e oohm
32	trinta e dois	treen-tah e doy-z
40	quarenta	kwah-ren-tah
50	cinqüenta	seen-kwen-tah
60	sessenta	seh-sen-tah
70	setenta	seh-ten-tah
80	oitenta	oy-ten-tah
90	noventa	noh-ven-tah
100	cem	say-m
101	cento e um	cen-too e oohm
200	duzentos	(doo-zayn-toosh)
300	trezentos	(treh-zayn-toosh)
400	quatrocentos	(kwa-tro-cen-toos)
500	quinhentos	(keen-nyientoosh)
600	seiscentos	(seh-eesh-cen-toosh]
700	setecentos	(seh-tay-cen-toosh
800	oitocentos	(oy-toh-cen-toosh
900	novecentos	(noh-vay-cen-toosh)
1000	mil	mee-oo
1100	mil e cem	mee-oo she-ing

1200	mil e duzentos	meal e doo-zayn-toosh
1300	mil e trezentos	(meal e treh-zayn-toosh)
2000	dois mil	(doh-eesh mil / (doo-ash meal)
1 million	um milhão	(ung mee-lyee-aung)
2 million	dois milhões	(doh-eesh mee-lyee-oingsh)
3 million	três milhões	(traysh mee-lyee-oingsh)
1 billion	um bilhão	(ung bee-lyee-aung)
1 billion	dois bilhões	(doh-eesh bee-lyee-oingsh)

Ordinal Numbers

Like most adjectives, ordinal numbers must match the gender and number of the noun they modify. When used before a feminine noun, ordinal numbers take an –a ending. They may also take plural endings. Ordinal numbers are generally placed before the noun they modify.

Feminine ending:

primeira senhora	the first lady
a primeira vez	the first time

Plural ending:

os primeiros jogos	the first games
os primeiros anos	the first years

The ordinal numbers are not commonly used to express the century in Portuguese. It is more typical for Portuguese speakers to refer to the century using cardinal numbers. For instance, the 21st century will often be referred to as "o século vinte e um". The century is also written using Roman numerals. For example, 21st century will be written as "o século XXI".

When indicating a century, Portuguese speakers would not normally use the ordinal numbers. Instead, it is more common to hear "o século vinte e um" (the century 21) than "o vigésimo primeiro século" (the 21st century). In Portuguese, centuries are written in Roman numerals. Hence, the 21st century is expressed as "o século XXI".

The cardinal numbers:

1st	primeiro	pre-may-roh	first
2nd	segundo	seh-goon-doh	second
3rd	terceiro	ter-say-roh	third

4th	quarto	ku-ar-toh	fourth
5th	quinto	keen-toh	fifth
6th	sexto	says-toh	sixty
7th	sétimo	seh-chee-moh	seventh
8th	oitavo	oy-tah-voh	eight
9th	nono	noh-nu	ninth
10th	décimo	dess-ee-moh	tenth
11th	décimo primeiro	dess-ee-moh-pre-may-roh	eleventh
12th	décimo segundo	dess-ee-moh-seh-goon-doh	twelfth
20th	vigésimo	vee-gess-ee-moh	twentieth
21st	vigésimo primeiro	vee-gess-ee-moh-pre-may-roh	twenty-first
22nd	vigésimo segundo	vee-gess-ee-moh-seh-goon-doh	twenty-second
30th	trigésimo	tree-gess-ee-moh	thirtieth
40th	quadragésimo	kuah-dra-gess-ee-moh	fourtieth
50th	qüinquagésimo	ku-een-ku-ah-gess-ee-moh	fiftieth
60th	sexagésimo	says-tah-gess-ee-moh	sixtieth
70th	septuagésimo	sep-too-ah-gess-ee-moh	seventieth
80th	octogésimo	ock-tah-gess-ee-moh	eightieth
90th	nonagésimo	noh-nah-gess-ee-moh	ninetieth
100th	centésimo	sen-tess-ee-moh	one hundredth
101st	centésimo primeiro	sem-tess-ee-moh-pre-may-roh	one hundred first

Chapter 5: Months, Days, and Seasons

In Portuguese, months of the year, days of the week, and seasons are not capitalized.

Os meses do ano (Months of the Year)

janeiro (zhah-NAY-doh)	January
fevereiro (feh-veh-DAY-doh)	February
março (MAH-soo)	March
abril (ah-BDEE-ooh)	April
maio (MY-oh)	May
junho (ZHOON-yoh)	June
julho (ZHOOL-yoh)	July
agosto (ah-GOH-stoh)	August
setembro (seh-TEHM-bdoh)	September
outubro (oh-TOO-bdoh)	October
novembro (noh-VEM-bdoh)	November
dezembro (deh-ZEM-bdoh)	December

Os dias da semana (Days of the Week)

domingo (doh-MING-goo)	Sunday
segunda-feira (seh-GOON-dah-FAY-dah)	Monday
terça-feira (TEH-sah-FAY-dah)	Tuesday
quarta-feira (KWAH-tah-FAY-dah)	Wednesday
quinta-feira (KEEN-tah-FAY-dah)	Thursday
sexta-feira (SEH-stah-FAY-dah)	Friday
sábado (SAH-bah-doh)	Saturday

As estações do ano (The Seasons of the Year)

primavera	spring
inverno	winter
verão	summer
outono	autumn/fall

Chapter 6: Telling Time, Date, and Year

To ask someone for the time of day, there are two ways of asking "What time is it?'

Que horas são?
Quantas horas são?

How to tell time

Telling time in Portuguese is very much similar to how you tell time in English. You will just have to say the hour, "e" (and), and the minutes.

For instance, to say it's 6:30 in Portuguese:

| São seis horas e trinta minutos. | It's six thirty. |

You can also choose to drop the hora and minutos:

São seis e trinta.

Take note of how "são", a form of "ser" (to be), is used to express time. Except when the hour is at one o'clock, you will always express time in the plural with the verb "são".

When the hour is exactly one o'clock, you will use the verb "é" which is another form of the verb "ser". Hence, you'll say "É uma hora" to mean "It's one o'clock." You will also use "é" to refer to specific time of day such as midnight or noon:

É meia-noite. (eh MAY-ah noh-ee-chee)   It's midnight.
É meio-dia.   (eh MAY-oh jee-ah)   It's noon.

To express an exact hour, you can say the hour using "são" and you may choose to end your statement with the expression "em ponto":

São oito horas.   São oito horas em ponto.
(It's eight o'clock.)   (It's eight o'clock sharp.)

To tell time at the half hour, you can use the words "e meia". For example:

São sete e meia.   It's seven thirty.

When the minutes are past the half-hour, it is quite common to state the number of minutes left before the coming hour and to use the preposition "para as" to introduce the coming hour.

For example:

5:42	São dezoito para as seis.	It's eighteen minutes to six.
8:50	São dez para as nove.	It's ten to nine.
9:45	São quinze para as dez.	It's fifteen to ten.

The 24-hour time format or precise time is more commonly used in Portuguese-speaking countries. In lieu of the time expression "am" and "pm", Portuguese speakers generally use time descriptions such as "da manhã", "da tarde"and "da noite" to indicate "in the morning", "in the afternoon", and "in the evening" respectively.

For example:

| 22:15 | São vinte e dois e quinze. | It's ten 15 PM. |
| 20:10 | São vinte e dez. | It's eight ten PM. |

To refer to the occurrence of an event at a particular time, you will need the preposition "às" (at) before the hour of the event.

For example:

O programa começa às 4:00 da tarde.
(The program starts at 4:00 in the afternoon.)

Time expressions:

quando?	when?
logo	soon
agora	now
mais tarde	later
antes	before
semana passada	last week
mês passado	last month
há um ano	a year ago
semana que vem	next week
ano que vem	next year
hoje	today
amanhã	tomorrow
ontem	yesterday
amanhecer	dawn
manhã	morning

meio-dia	noon
tarde	afternoon
fim de tarde	evening
anoitecer	dusk
noite	night
meia-noite	midnight
segundo(s)	second(s)
minuto(s)	minute(s)
hora(s)	hour(s)
dia(s)	day(s)
ano(s)	year(s)
mês(meses)	month(s)
semana(s)	week(s)

Writing dates in Portuguese

To express the date in Portuguese, you need to state the day before the month and the year. Hence: 26/12/2015.

To express it in the long format, you would need to use the preposition "de" which means "of". Thus, to state the preceding date in the long format, you would write "26 de dezembro de 2015".

Expressing the Year (Ano)

If the year you want to talk about is in the 20th century, you can say "mil novecentos e trinta e dois" to indicate the year 1932. If the year is in the current century (século), you will say "dois mil e quinze" to indicate the year 2015 for example.

Chapter 7: Weather and Seasons (Tempo/Clima e estações)

The Weather (Tempo/Clima)

When you want to make the most of your vacation time in a Portuguese-speaking place, you'll be very interested to know what the weather might be. Is it the best time to go to the beach? Is it going to rain? Will it be a sunny day? In this section, you will learn how to talk about the weather and ask questions about it.

A basic question you can ask to find out what the weather is like is "how's the weather today?"

Como está o tempo hoje?

Here are possible answers:

Está bonito.	It's beautiful.
Faz bom tempo.	It's good.
Está feio.	It's bad.
Está claro.	It's clear.
Está frio.	It's cold.
Está gelado.	It's icy.
Está nevando.	It's snowing.
Está geando.	It's frosty.
Está quente.	It's hot.
Está agradável.	It's nice.
Está ensolarado.	It's sunny.
Faz sol.	It's sunny.
Está ventando.	It's windy.
Está úmido.	It's humid.
Está chovendo.	It's raining.
Está nublado.	It's cloudy.

Useful weather terms:

a nuvem	the cloud
o ciclone	the cyclone
o terremoto	the earthquake
a enchente	the flood

a inundação	the flood
a neblina	the fog
o nevoeiro	the fog
a geada	the frost
o granizo	the hail
o furacão	the hurricane
o gelo	the ice
o raio	the lightning
a chuva	the rain
o arco-íris	the rainbow
a neve	the snow
o floco de neve	the snowflake
a temperature	the temperature
o trovão	the thunder
a tempestade	the thunderstorm
o vento	the wind
o guarda-chuva	the umbrella
o desabamento	the landslide

Seasons

primavera	spring
inverno	winter
outono	autumn/fall
verão	summer

Chapter 8 : Colors in Portuguese

Portuguese colors are adjectives and like other modifiers, they should match the gender and number of the noun they modify. When describing a feminine noun, adjectives normally must take an –a ending. When modifying plural nouns, numbers generally must add an –s ending to its singular form. The color blue, "azul" form the plural by dropping –l and adding –is.

Examples:

a maçã verde	the green apple
as maçãs verdes	the green apples
o livro vermelho	the red book
os livros vermelhos	the red books

vermelho	red
rosa	pink
laranja	orange
amarelo	yellow
verde	green
azul	blue
azul claro	light blue
roxo [rosho]	purple
violeta	violet
marrom	brown
marrom escuro	dark brown
preto	black
cinza	gray
branco	white
dourado	gold
prateado	silver

Chapter 9: Introductions

Knowing how to properly introduce yourself is important and, in this section, you will learn vital phrases you can use to meet new people and introduce yourself as well as your companion.

Introducing Yourself

To ask for the other person's name, you can use any of the following phrases:

What's your name?   Como você se chama?
                    Qual é o seu nome?

You can say your name in several ways:

Meu nome é _____. (My name is _____.)
(meh-ooh noh-mee eh___)

Muito prazer. (It's a pleasure to meet you.)

Pode me chamar de _____. (You can call me _____.)

Eu sou o/a _____. (I am _____.) (Use "o" if you're a male and "a" if you're a female.)

De onde você é?	Where are you from?
(Eu) sou do Canadá.	I'm from Canada.
(Eu) sou dos Estados Unidos.	I'm from the United States.
(Eu) sou canadense.	I'm a Canadian.
Sou Americano.	I'm an American.
Onde você mora?	Where do you live?
Moro no Canadá.	I live in Canada.
Moro nos Estados Unidos.	I live in the United States.
Quantos anos você tem?	How old are you?
Tenho trinta anos.	I'm thirty years old.
Com que você trabalha?	What is your job?
Trabalho como fotógrafo.	I work as a photographer.
Tenho que ir.	I have to go.

Introducing Others

Esta é a minha esposa.	This is my wife.
Este é o meu marido.	This is my husband.
Este é o meu amigo. *(es-chee eh ooh meh-ooh ah-mee-goo)*	This is my (male) friend.
Esta é a minha amiga. *(eh-stah eh ah ming-yah ah-mee-gah)*	This is my (female) friend.
Estes são os meus amigos. *(es-cheez sah-ooh ooz meh-ooz ah-mee-gooz)*	These are my friends. (mixed or all-male group)
Estas são as minhas amigas. *(eh-stahz sah-ooh ahz ming-yahz ah-mee-gahz)*	These are my friends. (all-female group)

In Portuguese, first names are called "primeiros nomes" while surnames are called "sobrenomes".

The words "Senhor" and "Senhora" are the equivalent of Mr. and Mrs or Miss in English. The definite article "o" and "a" (the) are used before "senhor" and "senhora". These titles are also more commonly used with the first names. Hence, you will likely come across such phrases as "a senhora Blanca" (the Mrs. Blanca).

Chapter 10: The Family

Your family is one of the natural subjects in any conversation about yourself. In this section, you will learn the Portuguese words for members of your family, how you can introduce each member, and present personal information about yourself.

O meu nome é Carlito.	My name is Carlito.
Tenho 26 anos.	I'm 26 years old.
Eu sou solteiro/solteira.	I'm single.
Sou o mais velho entre quatro filhos.	I'm the eldest among four children.
Tenho uma irmã e dois irmãos.	I have one sister and two brothers.
O nome da minha irmã é Carlota.	My sister's name is Carlota.
Ela tem 19 anos.	She is 19 years old.
Ela é mais jovem do que eu.	She is younger than me.
Ela gostaria de ser escritora.	She would like to be a writer.
Meu irmão mais novo tem 24 anos.	My younger brother is 24 years old.
Ele é programador.	He is a programmer.
Meu outro irmão tem 16 anos.	My other brother is 16 years old.
Ele é estudante.	He is a student.
Meu pai é advogado.	My father is a lawyer.
Minha mãe é secretária.	My mother is a secretary.

You can use the following words to describe your marital status. Take note that the words ending in –o are used if the speaker is a male while those ending in –a are used if the person talking is a female.

casado/casada	married
solteiro/solteira	single
divorciado/divorciada	divorced
separado/separada	separated
viúvo/viúva	widowed

Here are terms to describe your family members:

os pais	the parents
o marido (mah-DEE-do)	the husband
a mulher (mool-YEH)	the wife
o pai	the father

papai	dad
a mãe	the mother
mamãe	mom
os filhos	the children
o filho (FEEL-yo)	the son
a filha (FEEL-yah)	the daughter
o filho adotivo	the adopted son
a filha adotiva	the adopted daughter
o irmão (ee-MAH-ooh)	the brother
a irmã (ee-MAH)	the sister
o avô (ah-VAH)	the grandfather
vovô	grandpa
os avós	the grandparents
a avó (ah-VOH)	the grandmother
vovó	grandma
os netos	the grandchildren
o neto	the grandson
a neta	the granddaughter
o primo (PDEE-moh)	the cousin (male)
a prima (PDEE-mah)	the cousin (female)
o tio	the uncle
a tia	the aunt
o sobrinho	the nephew
a sobrinha	the niece
o padrasto	the stepfather
a madrasta	the stepmother
o sogro	the father-in-law
a sogra	the mother-in-law
o cunhado	the brother-in-law
a cunhada	the sister-in-law
o bisavô	the great-grandfather
a bisavó	the great-grandmother
o bisneto	the great-grandson
a bisneta	the great-granddaughter
meu irmão mais velho	my older brother
minha irmã mais nova	my younger sister
o caçula	the youngest (boy)
a caçula	the youngest (girl)
o menino	the boy

| a menina | the girl |

Chapter 11: Describing People

Knowing how to describe people's physical attributes and personality are important steps of your learning progress in Portuguese. You will find this knowledge invaluable in many situations.

Describing general features:

Ela/Ele é bonita/bonito.	She/He is pretty/handsome.
Ela é linda.	She's gorgeous.
Ela/Ele é feia/feio.	She/He is ugly.
Ela é atraente.	She is attractive.
Ele é careca.	He is bald.
Ele é meio careca.	He is a bit bald.
Ele usa peruca.	He uses a wig.
Ele é fortinho.	He is stocky.
Ele é musculoso.	He is muscular.
O meu amigo tem barba.	My friend has a beard.
bigode	moustache
cavanhaque	goatee.
gordinho	chubby
ombros largos	broad shoulders
cintura fina	slim waist
quadris largos	wide hips
nariz pontiagudo	pointed nose
nariz torto	crooked nose

Describing height and weight:

Ele tem altura mediana.	He has average height.
Ela é de peso médio.	She's of average weight.
Ele é alto.	He's tall.
Ela é alta.	She is tall.
Ele é baixo.	He's short.
Ela é baixa.	She is short.
Ele é gordo.	He's fat.
Ela é gorda.	She is fat.
Ele é magro.	He's thin.
Ele é magricelo.	He's skinny.
Ele é esbelto.	He's slim.

Describing hair, eyes, and skin color

Ela tem longos ecabelos loiros.	She has long blonde hair.
Ele tem cabelo preto e curto.	He has short black hair.
Ela é loira.	She's blonde.
Ela é ruiva.	She's red-haired.
Ela tem olhos castanhos.	She has brown eyes.
Ele é de pele escura.	He is dark-skinned.
Ela é de pele clara.	She is fair-skinned.
cabelo liso	straight hair
cabelo ondulado	wavy hair
cabelo ruivo	red hair
cabelo comprido	long hair
cabelo curto	short hair
cabelo tamanho médio	medium-length hair
cabelo encaracolado	curly hair
olhos castanhos	brown eyes
olhos verdes	green eyes
olhos azuis	blue eyes
olhos castanhos claro	light brown eyes
olhos castanhos escuro	dark brown eyes
cílios longos	long lashes

Describing personality:

Ele é amigável.	He is friendly.
Ela é divertida.	She is fun.
Ela é inteligente.	She is intelligent.
Ele/ela é tímido/tímida.	He/she is shy.
Ela é séria.	She is serious.
gentil	nice
quieto/quieta	quiet
inteligente	intelligent
paciente	patient
preguiçoso/preguiçosa	lazy
corajoso/corajosa	brave
sofisticado/sofisticada	sophisticated
trabalhador /trabalhadora	hardworking
engraçado/engracada	funny

pobre	poor
rico/rica	rich
simpatico/simpática	likable
velho/velha	old
jovem	young

Chapter 12: Asking for Directions

Getting around in a new place can be very challenging but if you know how to ask for and understand directions, you will most likely reach your travel destinations faster and easier. Here are important phrases and terms you need to know when asking for directions:

Estou perdido (male)/ perdida (female).	I'm lost.
Você pode me ajudar?	Can you help me?

Como vou _____?	How do I get to _____?
Como chego _____?	How do I get to _____?
___ponto de taxi (pon-toh djee ta-xi)	taxi stand
___à estação de trem (Br.)/comboios (Pt.) (AH ish-tah-SOW de trehm/ kohm-BOY-ohs)	train station
___à estação de ônibus (Br.) (AH ish-tah-SOW dje OH-nee-boos)	bus station
___à estação de autocarros (Pt.) (AH ish-tah-SOW duh ow-too-CAR-oosh)	bus station
___ao centro (Br)/à baixa (Pt.)	downtown
___ao hotel _____	the hotel _____
___a um bar/boate/festa	a bar/nightclub/party
___a um lan house	an Internet café
___correios (cohr-rey-oosh)	post office
___delegacia	police station
___pousada (poe-sah-dah)	guesthouse/inn
___hospital (osh-pi-tal)	hospital

Onde há muitos/muitas _____?	Where are there many _____?
___hotéis (oh-TEYSH)	hotels
___bares (barsh)	bars
___restaurantes? (resh-tau-RAN-t'sh)	restaurants
___lugares para visitar (Br)	sites to see
___sitios para visitar (Pt.)	sites to see

Onde é ___? (Ond-jee eh)	Where is ___?

Vire à esquerda. (VEER ah esh-KEHR-dah)	Turn left.

Vire à direita. (VEER ah dee-RAY-tah)	Turn right.

sempre em frente (Sempr' eim FREN-chee (Br.)/frente, Pt.)	Straight ahead.
Vá em frente. (Vah eim fren-the)	Walk straight ahead.
na direcção de ____ (nah dee-reh-SOWN duh)	towards the ____
antes de ____ (ant'sh deh)	before the ____
atrás (ah-trahsh)	behind
entre ____ e ____ (En-treh ____ e _)	between ____ and ____
próximo (Proh-see-mu)	next
depois de ____ (depoish deh)	past the ____
direito (dee-RAY-too)	right
esquerdo (esh-KEHR-doo)	left
endereço (en-deh-reh-su)	address
rua (ROO-ah)	street
quarteirão (koo-ahr-tey-roum)	block
mapa (mah-pah)	map
cruzamento (kroo-zah-MEN-too)	intersection
esquina (esh-kee-nah)	corner
subida (soo-BEE-dah)	uphill
descida (deh-SEE-dah, Br./desh-SEE-dah, Pt.)	downhill
norte (NOHR-chee or nortch, Br/NOHR-te, Pt.)	North
sul (sool)	South
leste (LESH-chee, Br./LESHt or ESHt, Pt.)	East
oeste (oh-EHS-chee, Br/oh-ESHt, Pt.)	West
semáforo (she-mah-foh-ru)	traffic light

Chapter 13: Getting Around

There are many modes of transportation but before you can use them in your visit to Portuguese-speaking places, you need to know the basic phrases to use to hire a taxi, take the bus/train, drive a car, or take a plane ride. Here are useful transportation words and phrases:

carro	car
taxi	taxi
ônibus (Br.) / autocarro (Pt.)	bus
trem (Br.) comboio (Pt.)	train
furgão/caminhonete	van
caminhão	truck/lorry
avião	airplane
metrô	underground/subway
eléctrico	tram
navio	ship
barco	boat
balsa	ferry
helicóptero	helicopter
linha aérea	airline
motocicleta	motorcycle
bicicleta	bicyle
carruagem (Br.), transporte(Pt.)	carriage
carrinho	trolley

Travelling by train or bus

Quanto custa uma passagem para_____?	How much is a ticket to_____?
Uma passagem para_____, por favor. (In Portugal, a ticket is "um bilhete".)	One ticket to_____, please.
Para onde vai o trem? (o comboio in Pt.)	Where does the train go?
Para onde vai o ônibus? (o autocarro in Pt.)	Where does the bus go?
Para onde é o autocarro/trem?	Where is the bus/train for?
Este autocarro/trem pára em_____?	Does this bus/train stop in___?
É directo?	Is it direct?
Há um lugar livre?	Is there a free seat?
Quero reservar um lugar.	I want to reserve a seat.

chegada	arrival

motorista	driver
partida	departure
compartimento de bagagem	baggage compartment
reserva	reservation
sanitário	toilet, bathroom
balcão	ticket office
lugar, assento	seat
um passe dum dia	a day pass
diariamente	daily
não entrar	no entry
sem saída	no exit

Taking a Taxi

Leve-me para____, por favor.	Please take me to____.
Pare aqui.	Stop here.
Siga aquele carro.	Follow that car.
OK, então vamos.	Ok, let's go then.

Travelling by Plane

Há algum vôo para____?	Is there a flight to____?
Quando são a chegada e a partida?	When is the arrival/departure?
Eu tenho passagem aberta.	I have an open ticket.
Qual o destino do senhor?	What is your destination, sir?
O senhor embarca às 13:30, tá?	You will board at 1:30, okay?
Boa viagem.	Have a nice trip.

agências de viagens	travel agencies
horário dos vôos	flight schedule
data da ida	departure date
data da volta	return date
ida e volta	round-trip ticket
somente ida	one-way ticket
avião	airplane
aeroporto	airport
corredor	aisle
comissário/comissária de bordo	flight attendant
classe econômica	economy class
primeira classe	first class

cabine	cabin
janela	window
bagagem	baggage
saída de emergência	emergency exit
a bagagem de mão	carry-on luggage
a bagagem despachada	checked luggage
o cartão de embarque	boarding pass
o portão	gate
a companhia aérea	airline
o vôo	flight
alfândega	customs
cinto de segurança	seatbelt

Chapter 14: Finding a Place to Stay

Some travellers simply want a comfortable place while some would prefer the most luxurious accommodations available. Whatever your preferences are, you need to know how to express yourself well in Portuguese to get the room you need.

Tem quartos disponíveis?	Do you have any available rooms?
Ficarei____ noite(s).	I will stay for ____ night(s).
Qual é o preço?	What is the price?
Peço desculpa, estamos cheios.	I'm sorry, we're full.
O quarto tem____(oo KWAHR-too teng)	Does the room come with ____
uma banheira? (oo-mah bah-NYAY-rah?)	a bathtub
um televisor? (oon teh-leh-VEE-zor?)	a television
um telefone? (teh-leh-FOW-nee,Br.) (oon teh-leh-FONE, Pt.)	a telephone
lençóis? (len-SOYSH)	bedsheets
ar condicionado	airconditioning

Vocês tem um cofre?	Do you have a safe?
O café da manhã está incluído?	Is breakfast included?
Há elevador?	Is there an elevator?

Chapter 15: Ordering Food in a Restaurant

You would certainly want to partake of a new city's specialty meals and local flavors so you need to practice important Portuguese dining phrases to be able to order your food the way you want them. Here are vital phrases to use when dining out:

crú (crew)	raw
mal passado (mahl pas-sah-du)	medium rate
bem passado (beim pas-sah-du)	well-done
garçom/garçonete (gar-som/gar-son-eh-tjee)	waiter
pedido (peh-djee-du)	order
prato (prah-tu)	dish
menu (meh-nu)	menu
prato principal (prah-tu prin-ci-pahl)	main course
bebida (beh-bee-dah)	drink
almoço (al-moh-su)	lunch
jantar (jan-tahr)	dinner
aperitivo (ah-per-ee-tee-vu)	appetizer
gorjeta (gohr-jeh-tah)	tip
mesa (meh-zah)	table
o cardápio	menu
meia porção (MEY-a dohz)	half portion
uma porção (OO-mah dohz)	full portion
refeição de preço fixo	fixed-price meal
à la carte	a la carte

Chapter 16: Shopping

Shopping for clothes, gifts, souvenirs, or essentials is a delightful activity but it can be very challenging if you have to do it in a foreign language. To help you get the most out of your buying adventure, here are vital phrases and terms you can use.

Shops to see:

a loja	the store
o shopping	the shopping center
os correios	the post office
o supermercado	the supermarket
o mercado	the market
a farmácia	the pharmacy
a loja de roupas	the clothing store
a livraria	the bookstore
a loja de ferramentas	the hardware store
a loja de sapatos	the shoe store
a loja de acessórios	the accessories store
a loja de brinquedos	the toys shop
o açougue	the butcher
a padaria	the bakery
a confeitaria	the pastry shop
a ótica	the optician
a loja de música	the music store

Useful Phrases:

Eu quero comprar_____.	I want to buy_____.
Estou procurando____.	I'm looking for___.
Estou procurando um relógio.	I'm looking for a watch.
Pode me ajudar?	Can you help me?
Quanto é_____?	How much is____?
Quanto é esta bolsa?	How much is this handbag?
Quanto é a camisa?	How much is the shirt?
Você tem____?	Do you have_____?
Tem____?	Do you have____?
Estou só a ver.	I'm just looking.
Quanto é este?	How much is this?
É muito caro.	It's too expensive.
Você tem um tamanho menor/maior?	Do you have a smaller/bigger size?

Você tem isto em tamanho médio?	Do you have this in medium size?
tamanho extra-grande	extra-large
tamanho grande	large size
tamanho pequeno	small size
Posso provar?	Can I try it?
Vou levar.	I will take it.
Onde está o caixa?	Where is the checkout?

At the supermarket:

Queria um_____.	I would like a_____.
uma quilo de maçãs	a kilo of apples
uma fatia de fiambre	a slice of ham
uma fatia de bolo	a piece of cake
uma caixa de chocolates	a box of chocolates
uma lata de atum	a can of tuna
um pacote de bolachas	a packet of biscuits

Store Signs:

Mulheres/Senhoras	Ladies
Homens/Senhores	Gentlemen
Empurre	Push
Puxe	Pull
Fechado	Closed
Aberto	Open
Horário de serviço	Store hours
Proibido estacionar	No parking
Proibido fumar!	No smoking!
Área para não-fumantes	Non- smoking area
Área para fumantes	Smoking area

Store vocabulary:

fechado	closed
o caixa	the checkout
carrinho de compras	shopping cart
carteira	wallet
cartão de crédito	credit card
dinheiro	money

moedas	coins
recibo	receipt
taxa	tax
caro	expensive
barato	cheap
cartão postal	postcard
selos	stamps
mercearias	groceries
maquiagem	make up
sapatos	shoes
roupas	clothes
ternos	men's suits

Daily supplies:

pão	bread
açúcar	sugar
massa/macarrão	pasta
manteiga	butter
arroz	rice
leite	milk
vinagre	vinegar
ovos	eggs
farinha	flour
sal	salt
mostarda	mustard
pimenta	pepper
café	coffee
chá	tea

Things to buy from a drug store:

a aspirina	the aspirin
a atadura	the bandage
o curativo adesivo	the band-aid
o algodão	the cotton
o barbeador elétrico	the electric shaver
o colírio	the eye drops
a escova de cabelos	the hairbrush
o batom	the lipstick

o cortador de unha	the nailclipper
o esmalte	the nail polish
a acetona	the nail polish remover
o analgésico	the painkiller
a água oxigenada	the peroxide
o aparelho de barbear	the shaver/ razor
o absorvente higiênico	the sanitary napkin
o xampu	the shampoo
a escova de dentes	the toothbrush
a espuma de barbear	the shaving foam
o sabonete	the soap
o desodorante em bastão	the deodorant (stick/roll-on)
o bronzeador	the suntan lotion
o papel higiênico	the toilet paper
a pasta de dentes	the toothpaste
o calmante	the tranquilizer

Chapter 17: Forming Sentences

In general, Portuguese basic word order is not much different from that of English: Subject-Verb-Object. You can use the same pattern to form statements, questions, and negative sentences.

Take a good look at this simple statement:

Subject	Verb	Direct Object
Ele	comprou	um relógio.
He	bought	a watch.

The basic statement can be expanded by including other words:

Subject	Verb	Direct Object	Indirect Object.
Ele	comprou	um relógio	para seu pai.
He	bought	a watch	for his father.

You can use the same structure to form an indirect question just don't forget to raise your intonation at the end to make it sound like a question.

Ele	comprou	um relógio	para seu pai?
Did he	buy	a watch	for his father?

Direct question:

By using question words before the subject-verb-object word order, you can easily make simple questions.

Onde	ele	comprou	um relógio	para seu pai?
Where	did he	buy	a watch	for his father?

Here are common question words and their English equivalent:

Onde (ohn-jee)	Where
Quem (kang)	Who
Qual (KWAH-ooh)	What/Which one
O que (ooh keh)	What

Quando (KWAHN-doh)	When
Quantos (KWAHN-tohs)	How many
Por que (poh-KEH)	Why
Quanto (KWAHN-toh)	How much
Como (KOH-moo)	How
De quem	Whose
Para onde	To where
A quem	To whom
Aonde	To where
Por que não	Why not
De onde	From where

Negative sentences

Negatives sentences express disagreement or denial. You can easily form a negative sentence by using the same word order and altering the meaning by placing a negative word before the verb.

Ele	não comprou	um relógio	para seu pai.
He	did not buy	a watch	for his father.

Eles	não comem	carne de porco
They	don't eat	pork meat.

Here are words you can use in forming negation:

não	no, don't
nada	nothing, (not) anything
nenhum(a)	no, none
ninguém	nobody, (not) anybody
nem sequer	not even
nem	nor
nem___nem	neither___nor
tampouco	neither, either
nunca, jamais	never, ever

Descriptive sentences

When it comes to sentences with adjectives, Portuguese word order radically differs from English. In Portuguese, adjectives are generally placed afer the noun they describe. In English, adjectives precede the noun they modify.

Subject	Adjective	Verb	Adjective
O carro	vermelho	é	caro.
The red	car	is	expensive.

Chapter 18: Nouns and Articles

The Articles (Artigos)

Articles indicate whether a noun is specific or not. Unlike articles in the English language, Portuguese articles should match both gender and number of the noun they modify.

Articles are grouped into definite and indefinite types. The definite articles are used in the same way that the article "the" is used in English. There are four forms of definite articles and indefinite articles to indicate the two genders and the plurality or singularity of the noun.

In general, articles are nearly always placed before a noun. Definite articles are more widely used in Portuguese than they are in the English language. They are commonly used before proper names like names of country, subjects, or even names of people.

Os Artigos Definidos (The definite articles)

Gender	English	Masculine	Feminine
Singular	the	o	a
Plural	the	os	as

Examples:

o gato	the cat
a cama	the bed
os céus azuis	the blue skies
as montanhas	the mountains

Os Artigos Indefinidos (The indefinite articles)

Gender	English	Masculine	Feminine
Singular	a, an,	um	uma
Plural	some	uns	umas

um livro	a book
uma biblioteca	a library
uns carros	some cars
umas coisas	some things

Nouns (Substantivos)

Nouns are names for persons, things, ideas, places, or events. Portuguese nouns are either masculine or feminine and singular or plural. In any case, the article and other modifiers should match the gender and number of the noun they modify.

Gender

In many cases, the gender of a noun may be easily identified just by looking at its ending. Here are the guidelines for determining whether a noun is masculine or feminine.

Masculine Nouns

Nouns ending in unstressed –o are generally masculine:

o marido	the husband
o ano	the year
o primo	the cousin
o carro	the car
o tio	the uncle
o amigo	the male friend

Tale note of these exceptions though: a foto (the photo), a tribo (the tribe)

Nouns which end with –m and –l are masculine

o jardim	the garden
o capim	the grass
o talharim	the noodles
o patim	the rollers
o trem	the train
o casal	the couple
o futebol	the football
o fossil	the fossil
o mel	the honey
o hospital	the hospital
o hotel	the hotel
o canil	the kennel
o painel	the panel, the picture

45

o papel	the paper
o perfil	the profile
o reptile	the reptile
o fuzil	the rifle
o anel	the ring
o lençol	the sheet
o caracol	the snail

Nouns ending with –r and –me are generally masculine.

o prazer	the pleasure
o ar	the air
o bar	the bar
o andar	the floor
o lar	the home
o humor	the humor
o motor	the motor
o colar	the necklace
o par	the pair, the couple
o ardor	the passion
o furor	the rage, the fury
o mar	the sea
o aspirador	the vacuum cleaner
o costume	the custom
o exame	the exam
o queixume	the lament
o lume	the light, the fire
o nome	the name
o cume	the summit, the top
o uniforme	the uniform
o legume	the legume
o volume	the volume

Some exceptions: a mulher (the woman), a dor (the pain), a colher (the spoon), a fome (the hunger), and a vexame (the humiliation).

Nouns with a stressed-a ending are generally masculine.

o imã	the magnet
o galã	the leading man

| o chá | the tea |
| o sofá | the sofa |

The exceptions include the nouns a maçã (the apple), a pá (the shovel) and a lã (the wool).

Some nouns ending in unstressed –a are masculine:

o planeta	the planet
o mapa	the map
o dia	the day
o guia	the guide

Some nouns ending with –ma are masculine nouns. These nouns are of Greek origin.

o clima	the climate
o sistema	the system
o programa	the program
o miasma	the decay
o drama	the drama

A few masculine nouns are flexible and may be used to refer to feminine nouns:

o animal	the animal
o indivíduo	the individual
o cônjuge	the spouse
o anjo	the angel

Feminine Nouns

Nouns with -são, -zão , –ção, –stão, or –gião endings are feminine:

a confusão	the confusion
a decisão	the decision
a evasão	the evasion
a ilusão	the illusion
a mansão	the mansion
a sessão	the session
a razão	the reason
a ilustração	the illustration

a imitação	the imitation
a intenção	the intention
a erudição	the erudition
a lição	the lesson
a nação	the nation
a posição	the position
a combustão	the combustion
a congestão	the congestion
a região	the region
a religião	the religion

A notable exception is the word "o coração" (the heart) which is a masculine noun.

Nouns ending with –gem and –cie are feminine:

a engrenagem	the car's gear
a malandragem	the cunning
a folhagem	the foliage
a ferragem	the hardware
a viagem	the journey
a margem	the margin
a paragem	the stop
a homenagem	the tribute
a meninice	the childhood
a imundície	the filth
a velhice	the old age
a planície	the plain
a superfície	the surface

Nouns ending with –ade and –ude are feminine.

a cidade	the city
a igualdade	the equality
a amizade	the friendship
a nacionalidade	the nationality
a piedade	the pity
a prioridade	the priority
a tranquilidade	the tranquillity
a universidade	the university
a virtude	the virtue

| a juventude | the youth |

Some feminine nouns may apply to masculine gender.

These feminine nouns are flexible and may be used to refer to the masculine gender:

a pessoa	the person
a besta	the beast
a criança	the child
a vítima	the victim
a testemunha	the witness

Nouns ending with e, z, and ão are either masculine or feminine and must be learned individually. You will find the following list useful:

Masculine nouns:

o arroz	the rice
o avião	the aeroplane
o cárcere	the prison
o cartaz	the bill, poster
o cheque	the cheque
o chicote	the whip
o desfile	the procession
o ente	the being
o envelope	the envelope
o escorregão	the slip-up
o esmalte	the nail polish
o gabinete	the office
o leste	the east
o limite	the limit
o monte	the hill, pile
o pão	the bread
o parente	the relative
o pé	the foot
o peixe	the fish
o recorte	the cutting, clip
o resgate	the ransom
o sangue	the blood
o satellite	the satellite
o traje	the dress, the suit

o travão	the brake
o trovão	the thunder
o vulcão	the volcano
o xadrez	the chess
o xerez	the sherry

Feminine Nouns

a escravidão	the slavery
a escuridão	the darkness
a frase	the sentence
a frente	the front
a gafe	the gaffe
a greve	the strike
a lente	the lens
a luz	the light
a maciez	the softness
a mão	the hand
a maré	the tide
a mercê	the mercy
a palidez	the paleness
a tarde	the afternoon
a vastidão	the immensity

Irregular Nouns

Some nouns have different forms for the masculine and feminine gender. These nouns mostly refer to professionals, family members or relatives, animals, nationalities, or titles.

Professions or nationalities

English	Masculine	Feminine
ambassador	o embaixador	a embaixatriz
poet	o poeta	a poetisa
hero	o herói	a heroina
champion	o campeão	a campeã
judge	o juiz	a juiza
European	o europeu	a europeia
Catalan	o catalão	a catalã

Jew	o judeu	a judia
German	o alemão	a alemã
citizen	o cidadão	a cidadã

Title, family/relatives, or animals

English	Masculine	English	Feminine
baron	o barão	baroness	a baronesa
count	o conde	countess	a condesa
duke	o duque	duchess	a duquesa
gentleman	o cavaleiro	lady	a dama
king	o rei	queen	a rainha
prince	o príncipe	princess	a princesa
brother	o irmão	sister	a irmã
father	o pai	mother	a mãe
father-in-law	o sogro	mother-in-law	a sogra
grandfather	o avô	grandmother	avó
husband	o marido	wife	a esposa
son-in-law	o genro	daughter-in-law	a genra
stepfather	o padrasto	stepmother	a madrasta
boy	o rapaz	girl	a rapariga (Pt)
monk	o monge	nun	a monja
actor	o ator	actress	a atriz
cock	o galo	hen	a galinha
cow/bull	o boi	cow/bull	a vaca
dog	o cão	bitch	a cadela/cachorra

Invariable Nouns

A few Portuguese nouns have similar forms for the male and female gender. The use of a definite or indefinite article before these nouns helps indicate their gender.

o/a estadunidense	the American
o/a artista	the artist
o/a burocrata	the bureaucrat
o/a cadete	the cadet
o/a canadense	the Canadian
o/a criança	the child
o/a colega	the classmate/colleague
o/a camarada	the comrade

o/a cliente	the customer/client
o/a democrata	the democrat
o/a motorista	the driver
o/a guia	the guide
o/a homicida	the homicide
o/a doente	the ill/invalid person
o/a indígena	the indigenous people
o/a intérprete	the interpreter
o/a gerente	the manager
o/a patriota	the patriot
o/a cobra	the snake
o/a estudante	the student
o/a suicida	the suicide
o/a taxista	the taxi driver
o/a tenista	the tennis player
o/a timorense	the Timorese
o/a jovem	the young person

The Plural Form

Portuguese nouns generally form the plural by varying the ending of their singular form. Here are important rules you should know in plural formation:

Nouns ending in –n, a vowel, or a diphthong (except those ending in–ão) form the plural by adding –s to their singular form.

Singular	Plural
o carro (the car)	os carros (the cars)
o germe (the germ)	os germes (the germs)
o amigo (friend)	os amigos (the friends)
a casa (the house)	as casas (the houses)
a mesa (the table)	as mesas (the tables)
a noite (the night)	as noites (the nights)
o prato (the plate)	os pratos (the plates)
o copo (the cup)	os copos (the cups)
a árvore (the tree)	as árvores (the trees)
o dia (the day)	os dias (the days)

o boi (the ox)	os bois (the oxen)
a lei (the law)	as leis (the laws)
o céu (the sky)	os céus (the skies)
o judeu (the Jew)	os judeus (the Jews)
o calendário (the calendar)	os calendários (the calendars)

Nouns ending with –m form their plural by replacing –m with –ns.

a viagem (the journey)	as viagens (the journeys)
o jardim (the garden)	os jardins (the gardens)
o trem (the train)	os trens (the trains)
o homem (the man)	os homens (the men)
a nuvem (the cloud)	as nuvens (the clouds)
a paisagem (the landscape)	as paisagens (the landscapes)

Nouns ending in –r or –z form their plural by adding -es

o cobertor (the blanket)	os cobertores (the blankets)
o cartaz (the poster)	os cartazes (the posters)
a mulher (the woman)	as mulheres (the women)
a luz (the light)	as luzes (the lights)
o rapaz (the boy)	os rapazes (the boys)
a atriz (the actress)	as atrizes (the actresses)
a colher (the spoon)	as colheres (the spoons)

Nouns ending in –s form their plural depending on the location of the stress. When the stress falls on the last syllable, nouns ending with -s form their plural by adding –es.

o mês (the month)	os meses (the months)
o deus (the god)	os deuses (the gods)
o país (the country)	os países (the countries)

Notice how the circumflex is dropped in the plural form. This rule is also applicable to nouns of nationalities.

o francês (the French)	os franceses (the French)
o inglês (the English)	os ingleses (the English)
o chinês (the Chinese)	os chineses (the Chinese)
o português (the Portuguese)	os portugueses (the Portuguese)

If the stress is on another syllable, nouns with –s ending have similar form for the singular and the plural.

o atlas (the atlas)	os atlas (the atlases)
o lapis (the pencil)	os lapis (the pencils)
o virus(the virus)	os virus (the viruses)
o alferes (the lieutenant)	os alferes (the lieutenants)

Nouns ending in –l form their plural depending on the placement of the stress. Here are the applicable rules for this nouns:

If the stress falls on the last syllable, nouns with –al ending form the plural by replacing –al with –ais.

o sinal (the sign)	os sinais (the signs)
o jornal (the newspaper)	os jornais (the newspapers)
a capital (the capital)	as capitais (the capitals)
o general (the general)	os generais (the generals)
o material (the material)	os materiais (the materials)

If the stress falls on the last syllable, nouns with –el ending form the plural by replacing –el with –eis and marking the –e with an acute accent to maintain the stress.

o hotel (the hotel)	os hotéis (the hotels)
o anel (the ring)	os aneis (the rings)
o papel (the paper)	os papéis (the papers)
o pastel (the pastry)	os pastéis (the pastry)

If the stress does not fall on the last syllable, nouns with –el ending form their plural by replacing –el with –eis.

| o telemóvel (the mobile phone) | os telemóveis (the mobile phones) |
| o túnel (the tunnel) | os túneis (the tunnels) |

If the stress falls on the last syllable, nouns with –il ending form the plural by dropping –l and adding s.

| o barril (the barrel) | os barris (the barrels) |
| o fuzil (the rifle) | os fuzis (the rifles) |

| o canil (the kennel) | os canis (the kennels) |
| o funil (the funnel) | os funis (the funnels) |

If the stress is elsewhere, nouns with –il ending form the plural by replacing –il with –eis.

o textil (the textile)	os têxteis (the textiles)
o fossil (the fossil)	os fósseis (the fossils)
o réptil (the reptile)	os répteis (the reptiles)

Some nouns ending in –l form their plural by adding –es:

| O consul (the consul) | os cônsules (the consuls) |
| O mal (the evil) | os males (the evils) |

When the stress is on the penultimate syllable, nouns ending in –x have the same form for the singular and the plural:

| o clímax (the climax) | os clímax (the climaxes) |
| o tórax (the thorax) | os tórax (the thoraxes) |

Nouns ending with -ão

Most nouns with –ão ending form their plural by replacing –ão with with an–ões ending.

o avião (the airplane)	os aviões (the airplanes)
o camião (the lorry)	os camiões (the lorries)
a obrigacão (the obligation)	as obrigacões (the obligations)
o limão (the lemon)	os limões (the lemons)
a canção (the song)	as canções (the songs)
a eleicão (the election)	as eleicões (the elections)
o gavião (the hawk)	os gaviões (the hawks)
a decisão (the decision)	as decisões (the decisions)
o avião (the airplane)	os aviões (the airplanes)
a televisão (the television)	as televisões (the televisions)
a nação (the nation)	as nações (the nations)

Some nouns ending with –ão form their plural by replacing –ão with –ães:

o escrivão (the scribe)	os escrivães (the scribes)
o cão (the dog)	os cães (the dogs)
o pão (the bread)	os pães (the breads)
o alemão (the German)	os alemães (the Germans)
o capitão (the captain)	os capitães (the captains)
o sacristão (the sacristan)	os sacristães (the sacristans)

Nouns which are unstressed on the last syllable change to plural by adding s.

o órgão (the organ)	os órgãos (the organs)
o sótão (the attic)	os sótãos (the attics)
o órfão (the orphan)	os órfãos (the orphans)

A few nouns ending with –ão also add –s to form the plural:

o irmão (the brother)	os irmãos (the brothers)
cidadão (the citizen)	os cidadãos (the citizens)
o cristão (the male Christian)	os cristãos (the male Christians)
a mão (the hand)	as mãos (the hands)

Words that are always in the Plural Form

The following words are always used in the plural:

as calças	pants
as costas	back (body part)
os óculos	glasses
os parabéns	congratulations
as férias	vacation

Expressing Possession in Portuguese

In English, the possessive is expressed by adding and apostrophe and s ('s) at the end of a noun. In Portuguese, you will use the preposition "de" (of) to denote possession.

For example, to say that a house belongs to Caterina:
A casa de Caterina (Caterina's house)

Chapter 19: Pronouns (Pronomes)

Pronouns are words used in place of a noun. There are six categories of pronouns in Portuguese: personal, possessive, relative, interrogative, demonstrative, and indefinite pronouns.

Personal Pronouns

There are five types of personal pronouns in Portuguese: subject, reflexive, prepositional, direct and indirect object pronouns.

Subject Pronouns (Pronomes Pessoais)

Subject pronouns or nominative pronouns act as doer of an action and come in several forms to indicate the number, gender, and person of the noun being replaced.

Portuguese subject pronouns are frequently dropped in sentences because the verb is formed in a way that you can easily tell the subject.

Here are the subject pronouns:

Singular	English	Portuguese
1st person	I	eu (EH-ooh)
2nd person	you	tu
	you	você (voh-SHE)
	you	o senhor, a senhora
3rd person	he, she, it	ele, ela (EH-lee/EH-la)
Plural		
1st person	we	nós (NOHZ)
2nd person	you	vós
	you	vocês
	you	os senhores, as senhoras
3rd person	they	eles, elas

The second person singular pronoun "tu" is only used in European Portuguese for informal conversations. In its place, Brazilian Portuguese uses the pronoun "você" as the standard word for "you". The pronouns "o senhor/a senhora" and their plural forms are the formal way to say "you" in European Portuguese and are commonly used when addressing older and important people in formal situations. The second person plural pronoun "vós" is now archaic and may only be found in literature and religious materials.

The third person plural "eles" and the second person plural "os senhores" may be used to refer to either an all-male group or a mixed group. Their feminine counterpart, on the other hand, may only be used when referring to an all-female group.

Examples:

Eu sou um artista.	I am an artist.
Você é um bom amigo.	You are a good friend.
Ela irá aderir ao passeio.	She will join the tour.
Eles são os funcionários diligentes.	They are hardworking employees.
Estamos sempre prontos para novos desafios.	We are always ready for new challenges.

Direct Object Pronouns

Direct object pronouns act as substitute for direct objects and are the recipient of the verb's action. For instance, in the sentence "She left him", "him" is the direct object of the verb "left".

English/Subject Pronoun	Direct Object Pronoun
Singular	
me	me
you (tu)	te
him, you (o senhor, você)	o
her, you (a senhora, você)	a
Plural	
us	nós
you (archaic)	vós
them (eles), you (os senhores, vocês)	os
them (elas), you (as senhoras, vocês)	as

Portuguese direct object pronouns generally appear before the verb but they may be found in other parts of the sentence.

The pronouns "o", "os", "a", and "as" are placed after the infinitive form of the verb. In this case, an "l" is added before the pronoun and a hypen is used to connect the verb to the pronoun. The verb itself must changes its form using these rules:

For verbs ending in –ar, the final "r" is dropped and an acute accent is placed on "a".

For verbs ending in –er, the final "r" is dropped and a circumflex is placed on "e".
For verbs ending in –ir, the final "r" is dropped.

Examples:

Se vê-lo.	If you see him.
Ela me conhece.	She knows me.
Eles vão levá-lo à escola.	They will take him to school.

Indirect Object Pronouns

Indirect pronouns are used to replace indirect objects in a sentence. They are commonly placed before the verb.

English/Subject Pronoun	Indirect Object Pronoun
Singular	
to me	me
to you (tu)	te
to him, to her, to you (você, o senhor, a senhora)	lhe
Plural	
to us	nos
to you (archaic)	vos
to them, to you (vocês, os senhores, as senhoras)	lhes

| Eu lhe comprei um presente. | I bought her a gift. |
| Ele me enviou um bilhete. | He sent me a ticket. |

Reflexive Pronouns

A reflexive pronoun refers the action back to the subject. It is used with a reflexive verb to indicate that the doer is also the recipient of the action. Reflexive pronouns are generally placed before the verb.

Here are the reflexive pronouns:

| Subject | English Reflexive | Reflexive |

eu	myself	me
tu (Port.)	yourself	te
ele, ela, você	himself, herself, yourself	se
nós	ourselves	nos
vós (archaic)	yourselves	vos
eles, elas, vocês	themselves, yourselves	se

Prepositional Pronouns

Prepositional pronouns are pronouns used as object of a preposition. In some cases, the pronoun and the preposition are contracted to form one word.

Here are the prepositional pronouns:

English	Portuguese
Singular	
me	mim
you	ti
you	você
you	o senhor, a senhora
him, her	ele, ela
him, her, it, you	si
Plural	
us	nós
(all of) you	vós
(all of) you	vocês
(all of) you	os senhores, as senhoras
them	eles, elas
them, (all of) you	si

A verificação está sobre mim.	The check is on me.
Isto não é sobre você.	This is not about you.

The preposition "com" (with) contracts with most prepositional pronouns to form a single word.

Take a look at the following table to see how the preposition "com" combines with pronouns:

English	Portuguese
Singular	
with me	comigo
with you	contigo
with you	com você
with you	com o senhor, com a senhora
him, her	com ele, com ela
with him, with her, with you	consigo
Plural	
with us	connosco (Brazil: conosco)
with (all of) you	convosco (archaic)
with (all of) you	com vocês
with (all of) you	com os senhores, com as senhoras
with them	com eles, com elas
with them, with (all of) you	consigo

Hence, to stay "with you" you'll have to say "contigo" instead of "com você".

Interrogative Pronouns

Interrogative pronouns are words you would use to ask questions. They are the equivalent of the English question words "who", "where", "when", "what", "which", "why", and "how". These pronouns are invariable in gender and number.

como?	how
onde?	where
por que?	why
qual?	which
quando?	when
quanto?	how much
que?	what

quem?	who
quem?	who (plural)

The interrogative pronouns "que" and "qual" both mean "what" in English but are used differently. While "que" always precedes a noun, this is not the case in "qual".

When used as a stand-alone question, question words using "que" such as "por que" or "o que" takes a circumflex accent. For example: "Eu não estava lá. Por quê?" (I wasn't there. Why?)

The question word "quem" (who) has a plural form, "quem", which is used when asking about two or more people.

The question word "onde" combines with "a" to form "aonde" meaning "at/to where". When used this way, it indicates direction.

Possessive Pronouns and Possessive Adjectives

Possessive pronouns and adjectives have identical forms. Both are used to express ownership but differ in their usage. Possessive pronouns replace a noun while possessive adjectives precede the noun they modify. Both must match the gender and number of the possessed object.

Possessive Pronouns and Adjectives

Possessor	Possessed object			
	Feminine		Masculine	
	Singular	Plural	Singular	Plural
eu	minha	minhas	meu	meus
tu	tua	tuas	teu	teus
ele, ela, você	sua	suas	seu	seus
nós	nossa	nossas	nosso	nossos
vós	vossa	vossas	vosso	vossos
eles, elas, vocês	sua	suas	seu	seus

Examples:

O meu cão é corajoso e forte.	My dog is brave and strong.
Os meus cães são fortes e corajosos.	My dogs are brave and strong.
O cão é meu.	The dog is mine.

| Os cães são meus. | The dogs are mine. |

Demonstrative Pronouns and Demonstrative Adjectives

Demonstrative words are used to point to a thing or person or indicate distance between a speaker and another person or object.

Demonstrative Pronouns

isto	this
estes	these
aquilo	that (over there)
aqueles	those (over there)
isso	that
esses	those

Isto é o meu saco.	This is my bag.
O que são estes?	What are these?

Demonstrative Adjectives

A demonstrative adjective modify a noun and must agree with its gender and number.

English	Masculine	Feminine
this	este	esta
these	estes	estas
that	esse	essa
those	esses	essas
that (over there)	aquele	aquela
those (over there)	aqueles	aquelas

Examples:

Estes sacos são meus.	These bags are mine.
Aquela casa é sua.	That house is yours.

Indefinite Pronouns

Indefinite pronouns are words that refer to an identifiable but non-specific things or people.

alguém	somebody/anybody
ninguém	nobody/no one
algum/alguns	some/any
nenhum	none (male)
alguma(s)	some/any
nenhuma	none (female)
alguma coisa	something
algo	something
nada	nothing
bastante	a lot
certo(s)/certa(s)	certain
cada	every
mais	more
menos	less
muito/muita	much
pouco/pouca	little
muitos/muitas	many
poucos/poucas	few
qualquer	any, any one
tantos/tantas	so many
tanto/tanta	so much
tal/tais	such
todos/todas	every/all
todo/toda	whole/entire
tudo	everything
uns/umas	some/about
vários/várias	several

Examples:

Alguns não estão interessados.	Some are not interested.
Alguém disse à polícia.	Somebody told the police

Chapter 20: Adjectives

Adjectives are words that modify or describe a noun or a pronoun. Adjectives must agree with the gender and number of the word they modify. Portuguese regular adjectives usually end in –e, -o, or a consonant.

Adjectives ending in –o can have four forms.

Take for example the adjective pequeno (small):

	singular	plural
masculine	pequeno	pequenos
feminine	pequena	pequenas

Examples:

casa pequena (small house)
carro pequeno (small car)
casas pequenas (small houses)
carros pequenos (small cars)

Adjectives that end in –e can take two forms – one form for both masculine and feminine in plural and singular.

humilde (humble)

	singular	plural
masculine	humilde	humildes
feminine	humilde	humildes

Examples:

homem humilde	humble man
senhora humilde	humble lady
homens humildes	humble men
mulheres humildes	humble women

Portuguese adjectives are generally placed after the noun. Some adjectives, however, are commonly placed before the noun. This includes irregular adjectives like "mau" (bad) and "bom" (good). Some adjectives such as "grande" or "bom" mean differently depending on their placement.

Examples:

O grande herói sacrificou sua vida para o seu país.
(The great hero sacrificed his life for his country.)

A casa grande pertence ao meu amigo.
(The big house belongs to my friend.)

Minha mãe é uma pessoa generosa.
(My mother is a generous person.)

Irregular Adjectives

Irregular adjectives are descriptive words that deviate from the regular patterns that govern adjective forms.

Adjectives ending in –m or –ão are irregular adjectives and uses distinct forms to express the number and gender of the word they modify.

Adjectives with –m ending have similar form for both masculine and feminine gender and form their plural by changing their ending from –m to –n and adding "s".

An example of this deviation is the adjective "jovem" (young).

	singular	plural
feminine	jovem	jovens
masculine	jovem	jovens

Adjectives ending in –ão generally have four forms. Take for instance the adjective "são" (sane) which means healthy or sane.

	singular	plural
feminine	sã	sãs
masculine	são	sãos

Most Common Adjectives

zangado	angry

mau	bad
bonito	beautiful
barato	cheap
limpo	clean
fechado	closed
frio	cold
diferente	different
difícil	difficult
directo	direct
cedo	early
fácil	easy
longe	far
amigável	friendly
bom	good
pesado	heavy
sério	serious
quente	hot, warm
importante	important
comprido	long
longa	long
casado	married
natural	natural
perto	near
novo	new
amável	nice, lovely
velho	old
aberto	open
lotado	packed with people
gentil	polite
pobre	poor
rico	rich
triste	sad
baixo	short
curto	short
simples	simple
lento	slow
pequeno	small
doce	sweet
alto	tall

feio	ugly
morno	warm
bem	well
pior	worse
o pior	worst
incorrecto	wrong

Chapter 21: Verbs

Verbs are words that denote a condition or action. Portuguese verbs convey important information such as the person and gender of the subject. Most verbs fall under the three main verb types and must follow the prescribed endings for each verb group. They are the –ar verbs (first conjugation), -er verbs (second conjugation), and –ir verbs (third conjugation).

Verb Moods

There are four verb moods in Portuguese: the indicative, the subjunctive, the imperative, and the conditional.

The indicative mood is the most common mood. It denotes action that is happening in the present, have happened in the past, and will happen in the future.

The subjunctive mood expresses a wish or an action that may or may not happen.

The imperative mood is used to convey commands.

The conditional mood indicates the possibility for an event to happen subject to certain conditions.

Verb Tenses

Tenses tell something about the time of an event or action's occurrence. There are different verb tenses under each mood.

Conjugating Portuguese Verbs

For verbs to be able to convey information on the gender and number of the subject, it must use appropriate endings for each subject. This is done by conjugating a verb or changing its ending in accordance with the prescribed conjugation table for each verb group. To conjugate a verb, you have to obtain the verb stem by dropping the –ar, -er, or –ir endings in its infinitive form and adding the correct personal endings.

For example, to conjugate the verb cantar (to sing), you have to obtain the verb stem which is "cant". To say "I sing", you will need to add the personal ending –o to the verb stem. Hence, "(Eu) canto" (I sing).

Here are conjugation tables for each verb group in 4 basic tenses in the indicative mood:

-ar verbs

Subject	English	Present	Simple Past	Future	Imperfect
eu	I	-o	-ei	-arei	-ava
tu (Portugal)	you (informal)	-as	-ste	-arás	-avas
ele, ela, você	he, she, you	-a	-ou	-ará	-ava
nós	we	-amos	-ámos	-aremos	-ávamos
vós (archaic)	you (informal)	-ais	-astes	-areis	-áveis
eles, elas, vocês	they, you	-am	-aram	-arão	-avam

Example: cantar - to sing

Present tense Eu canto. (I sing.)
Ele canta. (He sings.)

Simple past Eu cantei. (I sang.)
Eles cantaram. (They sang.)

Future Nós cantaremos. (We will sing.)
Eu cantarei. (I will sing.)

Imperfect Você cantava. (You used to sing).
Eu cantava. (I used to sing.)

-er verbs

Subject	English	Present	Simple Past	Future	Imperfect
eu	I	-o	-i	-erei	-ia
tu (Portugal)	you (informal)	-es	-este	-erás	-ias
ele, ela, você	he, she, you	-e	-eu	-erá	-ia
nós	we	-emos	-emos	-eremos	-íamos
vós (archaic)	you (informal)	-eis	-estes	-ereis	-íeis
eles, elas, vocês	they, you	-em	-eram	-erão	-iam

Example: escrever (to write)

Present tense   Eu escrevo. (I write.)
                 Ela escreve. (She writes.)

Simple past   Eu escrevi. (I wrote.)
                 Elas escreveram. (They wrote.)

Future   Nós escreveremos. (We will write.)
                 Eu escreverei. (I will write.)

Imperfect   Você escrevia. (You used to write).
                 Eu escrevia. (I used to write.)

-ir verbs

Subject	English	Present	Simple Past	Future	Imperfect
eu	I	-o	-i	-irei	-ia
tu (Portugal)	you (informal)	-es	-iste	-irás	-ias
ele, ela, você	he, she, you	-e	-iu	-irá	-ia
nós	we	-imos	-imos	-iremos	-íamos
vós (archaic)	you (informal)	-is	-istes	-ireis	-íeis
eles, elas, vocês	they, you	-em	-iram	-irão	-iam

Example: partir (to leave)

Present tense   Eu parto. (I leave.)
Você parte. (You leave.)

Simple past   Eu parti. (I left.)
Nós partimos. (They left.)

Future   Nós partiremos. (We will leave.)
Eu partirei. (I will leave.)

Imperfect   Vocês partiam. (You used to leave.)
Eu partia. (I used to leave.)

The Present Progressive Tense

The present progressive tense is a compound verb which is formed by using the present tense of "estar" (to be) and the present participle form of the verb. It is the equivalent of "to be+_ing" in English.

The present participle form of the verb is invariable in gender and number and only has one form for each verb group:

-ar verbs   -ando
-er verbs   -endo
-ir verbs   -indo

The verb "estar" uses the following table to express the present tense:

Subject	English	estar
eu	I	estou
tu (Pt.)	you (inf.)	estás
ele/ela/você	he/she/you (formal)	está
nós	we	estamos
vós (archaic)	you (inf. plural)	estais
eles/elas/vocês	they/you	estão

Examples:

Eu estou cantando.	I am singing.
Nós estamos cantando.	We are singing.
Você está escrevendo.	You are writing.
Eu estou escrevendo.	I am writing.
Nós estamos partindo.	We are leaving.

| Eu estou partindo. | I am leaving. |

The Past Participle

The past participle form of the verb is combined with the verb "ter" (to have) to form compound verbs. They can also function as adjectives and vary in form to reflect the number and gender of the word they modify.

The past participle has the following endings for the three verb groups:

-ar verbs   -ado
-er verbs   -ido
-ir verbs   -ido

Some verbs, however, have irregular forms in the past participle including the following:

Infinitive	Past Participle	English
vir (to come)	vindo	come
por (to put)	posto	placed
cobrir (to cover)	coberto	covered
ver (to see)	visto	seen
morrer (to die)	morto	dead
abrir (to open)	aberto	opened
fazer (to do)	feito	done
escrever (to write)	escrito	written
dizer (to say)	dito	said

On the other hand, some verbs have irregular past participle form as adjectives but follow the regular pattern when functioning as a verb:

Infinitive	Past Participle		Adjective	
aceitar (to accept)	aceitado	accepted	aceito	accepted
pagar (to pay)	pagado	paid	pago	paid
nascer (to be born)	nascido	born	nato	born
gastar (to spend)	gastado	spent	gasto	spent
limpar (to clean)	limpado	cleaned	limpo	cleaned
acender (to light)	acendido	lit	aceso	lit
juntar (to join)	juntado	joined	junto	together

| ganhar (to win) | ganhado | won | ganho | won |
| fritar (to fry) | fritado | fried | frito | fried |

Past participle form as adjective:

os momentos furtados   the stolen moments
o jogo perdido   the lost game

Compound Verbs

A compound verb is formed by combining the verb "ter" (to have) with the past participle of the verb. By conjugating "ter", an irregular verb, you can easily construct compound verbs to express different tenses and moods.

Indicative Mood:

Subject	Present	Preterit	Future	Imperfect
eu	tenho	tive	terei	tinha
tu (Pt.)	tens	tiveste	terás	tinhas
ele/ela/você	tem	teve	terá	tinha
nós	temos	tivemos	teremos	tínhamos
vós (archaic)	tendes	tivestes	tereis	tínheis
eles/elas/vocês	têm	tiveram	terão	tinham

Subjunctive Mood:

Subject	Present	Future	Imperfect
eu	tenha	tiver	tivesse
tu (Pt.)	tenhas	tiveres	tivesses
ele/ela/você	tenha	tiver	tivesse
nós	tenhamos	tivermos	tivéssemos
vós (archaic)	tenhais	tiverdes	tivésseis
eles/elas/vocês	tenham	tiverem	tivessem

Conditional and Imperative Moods:

Subject	Conditional	Imperative
eu	teria	-
tu (Portugal)	terias	tem
ele, ela, você	teria	tenha
nós	teríamos	tenhamos
vós (archaic)	teríeis	tende
eles, elas, vocês	teriam	tenham

Participle Forms	
Present Participle	tendo
Past Participle	tido

To use the verb "vender" (to sell) with "ter" to form the different compound perfect tenses, study the following sentences:

Present perfect	Eu tenho vendido o meu carro.	I have sold my car.
Past perfect	Eu tinha vendido o meu carro.	I had sold my car.
Future perfect	Eu terei vendido o meu carro.	I will have sold my car.
Conditional perfect	Eu teria vendido o meu carro.	I would have sold my car.

The Imperative Mood

The imperative mood is used to directly express a command. Following is the conjugation table for the different verb groups in the imperative:

Subject	English	-ar verbs	-er verbs	-ir verbs
tu (Pt.)	you (informal, sing.)	-a	-e	-e
você	you (singular)	-e	-a	-a
nós	we	-emos	-amos	-amos
vós (archaic)	you (informal, plural)	-ai	-ei	-i
vocês	you (plural)	-em	-am	-am

Examples:

(Você) fale!	Speak!
Sente!	Sit!
Pare!	Stop!

Subjunctive Mood

The subjunctive mood is used in hypothetical statements to express a wish, possibility, opinion, obligation, emotion, judgment, or action.

The following endings are used to form the different tenses in the subjunctive:

-ar Verbs

Subject	English	Present	Imperfect	Future
eu	I	-e	-asse	-ar
tu (Pt.)	you (inf.)	-es	-asses	-ares
ele/ela/você	he, she, you	-e	-asse	-ar
nós	we	-emos	-ássemos	-armos
vós (archaic)	you (inf.)	-eis	-ásseis	-ardes
eles/elas/vocês	they, you	-em	-assem	-arem

-er verbs

Subject	English	Present	Imperfect	Future
eu	I	-a	-esse	-esse
tu (Pt.)	you (inf.)	-as	-esses	-esses
ele/ela/você	he, she, you	-a	-esse	-esse
nós	we	-amos	-êssemos	-êssemos
vós (archaic)	you (inf.)	-ais	-êsseis	-êsseis
eles/elas/vocês	they, you	-am	-essem	-essem

-ir verbs

Subject	English	Present	Imperfect	Future
eu	I	-a	-isse	-isse
tu (Pt.)	you (inf.)	-as	-isses	-isses

ele/ela/você	he, she, you	-a	-isse	-isse
nós	we	-amos	-íssemos	-íssemos
vós (archaic)	you (inf.)	-ais	-ísseis	-ísseis
eles/elas/vocês	they, you	-am	-issem	-issem

Examples:

Quando ele chegar, chame a polícia.	As soon as he arrives, call the police.
Eu sugiro que ele coma frutas frescas.	I suggest that he eats fresh fruits.

Reflexive Verbs

Reflexive verbs point to the same subject (doer) and receiver (object). They require a reflexive pronoun, which may be placed before the verb or attached to the verb with a hypen. These verbs are conjugated in the same way that you would conjugate other verbs.

Examples:

Ele se lembra.	He remembers.
Ele lembra-se.	He remembers.
Eu me lavo.	I wash myself.
Eu lavo-me.	I wash myself.

Common reflexive verbs:

Reflexive Verb	Meaning
machucar-se	to bruise
pentear-se	to comb
cortar-se	to cut
vestir-se	to dress
enxugar-se	to dry off
sentir-se	to feel
levantar-se	to get up
servir-se	to help oneself
deitar-se	to lie down
lembrar-se	to remember
sentar-se	to sit down

| lavar-se | to wash up |

Ser and Estar

The verbs "ser" and "estar" are two of the most commonly used verbs. While they both translate to the English verb "to be", they have distinct uses.

Ser

You use the verb "ser" when referring to permanent or long-term conditions or characteristic. It is used for expressing the time of day and for associating people with their occupation.

Ele é casado.	He is married.
Ele é amável.	He is kind.
Ela é uma doutora.	She is a doctor.
São duas horas.	It's two o'clock.

Conjugation table for "ser"

Subject	Present	Perfect Past	Futuro	Imperfect
eu	sou	fui	seria	era
tu (Port.)	és	foste	serás	eras
ele/ela/você	é	foi	sera	era
nós	somos	fomos	seremos	éramos
vós (archaic)	sois	fostes	series	éreis
eles/elas/vocês	são	foram	serão	eram

Estar

You use "estar" to indicate temporary characteristics or state of being such as weather conditions. When used with an adjective, it denotes a temporary quality.

Ela está muito feliz.	She is very happy.
Eles estão doentes.	They are sick.
Está chovendo.	It is raining.

Conjugation table for "estar"

Subject	Present	Perfect Past	Futuro	Imperfect
eu	estou	estive	estarei	estava
tu (Port.)	estás	estiveste	estarás	estavas
ele/ela/você	está	esteve	estará	estava
nós	estamos	estivemos	estaremos	estávamos
vós (archaic)	estais	estivestes	estareis	estáveis
eles/elas/vocês	estão	estiveram	estarão	estavam

The Passive Voice

In the passive voice, the action is done to the subject in contrast with the active voice where the subject is the doer of the action. The passive voice is formed in Portuguese by using the verb "ser" with the main verb's past participle.

Example:

| Ele foi examinado. | He was examined. |
| Eu fui acertado por uma bola. | I was hit by a ball. |

Most Commonly Used Verbs

ser	to be
ter	to have
ir	to go
estar	to be
fazer	to do
ver	to see
olhar	to look

poder	to be able to
pôr	to put
vir	to come
cantar	to sing
sentar	to sit
comer	to eat
beber	to drink
dormir	to sleep
estudar	to study
aprender	to learn
comprender	to understand
saber	to know
ler	to read
esperar	to wait
jogar	to play
escrever	to write
dizer	to say, tell
pedir	to ask (for something)
encontrar	to find
perder	to lose
ouvir	to hear
amar	to love
viver	to live
vender	to sell
comprar	to buy
abrir	to open
fechar	to close

Chapter 22: Adverbs (Advérbios)

Adverbs are words that modify an adjective, a verb, and another adverb. Portuguese adverbs are invariable.

Many adverbs are formed by adding the –mente ending to the adjective's feminine form. Take for instance the adjective aberto which means open. To change it to an adverb which means openly, you would simply add –mente to its feminine form "aberta" to come up with the adverb "abertamente" (openly).

The different types and forms of adverbs indicate time, quantity, place, mode, intensity, doubt, denial, affirmation, and exclusivity.

Following are the most commonly used adverbs:

Adverbs of Time

sempre	always, constantly
enfim	anyway
antes	before
cedo	early
nunca	ever, never
primeiro	firstly
dantes	formerly
antigamente	formerly
logo	immediately, shortly
tarde	late
já não	not any more
já	now, already
agora	now, nowadays
ainda	still, yet
então	then, so
hoje	today
amanhã	tomorrow
ontem	yesterday

Comprei uma camisa **ontem**. I bought a shirt yesterday.
Ela foi para casa cedo. She went home early.

Adverbs of Place

Portuguese	English
acima	above
adiante (de)	ahead
detrás (de)	behind
atrás (de)	behind, at the rear
abaixo	below
longe (de)	far from
aqui	here
cá	here
dentro (de)	inside
fora (de)	outside
perto (de)	near, next to around the corner
lá	over there (far)
alí	over there (close)
aí	there, then (Br.)
debaixo	under
	underneath

Você pode ficar aqui. (You can stay here.)
Seus amigos estão andando atrás de você. (Your friends are walking behind you.)

Adverbs of Manner

sobretudo	above all
efetivamente	actually
como	as, like, the way like
mal	badly
melhor	better
facilmente	easily
principalmente	mainly

depressa	quickly
rapidamente	quickly
devagar	slowly
assim	so, therefore, this way
bem	well
pior	worse

Ele **rapidamente** disse adeus. He quickly said goodbye.
Ela caminha **como** uma princesa. She walks like a princess.

Adverbs of quantity and intensity

Portuguese	English
quase (de)	almost
quanto (de)	as much
tanto	as much, too much
bastante	enough, a lot, too much
menos	less, minus
pouco	little
mais	more, plus
tão (de)	so much
demasiado (de)	too much
muito	very, much, too, too much

Ela era **mais** animada. She was more excited.
Ele estava **muito** desapontado. He was very disappointed.

Adverbs of Affirmation

Portuguese	English
decerto	certainly
certamente	certainly, for sure
realmente	really
sim	yes

As crianças ficam **realmente** felizes. The children are really happy.
Ele é **certamente** esperançoso. He is certainly hopeful.

Adverbs of Denial

Portuguese	English
nem	neither, nor
jamais	never ever
nunca	never, ever
não	no, don't

Ele não era **nunca** leal. He was never loyal.
Não vá à festa. Don't go to the party.

Adverbs of Doubt

Portuguese	English
talvez	may, maybe, perhaps
se calhar	may, maybe, perhaps
provavelmente	probably

Ele **provavelmente** está doente. He is probably sick.

Adverbs of Exclusivity

apenas	just, only
só	just, only
somente	just, only
unicamente	just, only
senão	otherwise

Estamos tendo cuidado **somente** em torno. We are only looking around.

Adverbial Phrases

Portuguese	English

de facto (PT)	actually
de fato (BR)	actually
de novo	again, one more time
a sós	alone
de lado	beside
por acaso	by chance
à vontade	comfortably
à toa	idly
com efeito	effectively
em resumo	in conclusion
às escuras	in the dark
em vão	in vain
actualmente	nowadays
de vez em quando	from time to time, now and then
a cada passo	often
como deve ser	properly
ao acaso	randomly
às direitas	right, well
por alto	roughly
às vezes	sometimes
em breve	soon, shortly
com certeza	surely, certainly
de baixo	under

Ele **às vezes** ficou zangado com ele mesmo. He was sometimes angry at himself.
Ele ganhou **por acaso**. He won by chance.

Chapter 23: Prepositions

Prepositions are words that link other words in a phrase or sentence. Portuguese prepositions are always placed before the noun.

Following are the most commonly-used prepositions:

Prepositions of location

entre	(in) between
acima (de)/por cima(de)	above
ao longo(de)	along
em redor(de)	around
à	at
atrás (de)	behind
debaixo (de)	below, under
em frente(de)	in front (of)
à frente(de)	in front of
no meio(de)	in the middle (of), in the center (of)
dentro (de)	in, inside
em	in, on, at
perto (de)	near
ao lado (de)	next (to)
em cima (de)	on top (of)
fora (de)	outside (of)

Ele estava ficando **à frente do** edifício. He was staying in front of the building.
O carro está estacionado **perto do** portão.   The car is parked near the gate.

Prepositions of Time

depois (de)	after
antes (de)	before
entre	between
durante	during, for
dentro (de)	in
em+months	in+months

86

em+year	in+year
em+day	on the +day+month/on+month+day
desde	since
até	until

Ele esperou **até** ficar escuro. He waited until it was dark.
Ele nasceu **em** 1988. He was born in 1988.
O meu aniversário é **em** 24 Janeiro. My birthday is on January 24.

Prepositions of direction

para	for, to
de	from
sobre	over
através (de)	through
a	to

Ela veio **de** Paris. She came from Paris.
O menino saltou **sobre** a cerca. The boy jumped over the fence.

Other Prepositions

sobre	about
conforme, segundo	according (to)
contra	against
por causa (de)	because of
menos	but, except
a respeito (de)	concerning, regarding
por	for, because of
para	for, in order to
de	from (origin, possession)
apesar (de)	in spite of, despite
em vez (de)	instead (of)
junto (com)	together (with)
com	with
sem	without

Ele veio **com** os seus amigos.   He came with his friends.
O seu pai era **contra** a sua idéia.   His father was against his idea.

Prepositional Contractions

Some prepositions combine with definite and indefinite articles into one contracted form:

Prepositions	with o/a	with os/as	with um/uma	with uns/umas
a (to/at)	ao, à	aos, às		
em (in/on)	no, na	nos, nas	num, numa	nuns, numas
de (of/from)	do, da	dos, das	dum, duma	duns, dumas
para (for)	pro, pra	pros, pras	prum, pruma	pruns, prumas
por (for)	pelo, pela	pelos, pelas	pelum, peluma	peluns, pelumas

Examples:

Eles foram ao parque.   They went to the park.
Ele está no meio da controvérsia. He is in the middle of the controversy.

Chapter 24: Vocabulary

Occupation

o escritor	the writer
o garcon	the waiter
o veterinário	the veterinarian
o coveiro	the undertaker
o tradutor	the translator
o treinador	the trainer
o jornalista	the the journalist
o taxista	the taxi driver
o camelô	the street vendor
o locutor	the speaker
o soldado	the soldier
o cantor	the singer
a secretária	the secretary
o cientista	the scientist
o marinheiro	the sailor
o aposentado	the retired
o repórter	the reporter
o psicólogo	the pyschologist
o programador	the programmer
o professor	the professor
o presidente	the president
o carteiro	the postman
o político	the politician
o polícia	the policeman
o encanador	the plumber
o piloto	the pilot
o fisioterapeuta	the physiotherapist
o fotógrafo	the photographer
o farmacêutico	the pharmacist
o pintor	the painter
a nutricionista	the nutritionist
o enfermeiro	the nurse

o músico	the musician
o modelo	the model
a parteira	the midwife
o mecânico	the mechanic
o gerente	the manager
a doméstica	the maid
o bibliotecário	the librarian
o palestrante	the lecturer
o advogado	the lawyer
o juiz	the judge
o intérprete	the interpreter
o caçador	the hunter
a dona-de-casa	the housewife
o cabeleireiro	the hairdresser
o lixeiro	the garbage collector
o pescador	the fisherman
o bombeiro	the fireman
o agricultor	the farmer
o engenheiro	the engineer
o eletricista	the electrician
o pedagogo	the educator
o condutor	the driver
o médico	the doctor
o detetive	the detective
a projetista	the designer
o dentista	the dentist
o decorador	the decorator
o dançarino	the dancer
o chefe de cozinha	the chef
o talhante / açougueiro	the butcher
o pedreiro	the bricklayer
o guarda costas	the body guard
o biólogo	the biologist
o barbeiro	the barber
o banqueiro	the banker
o padeiro	the baker
o artista	the artist

o arquiteto	the architect
a atriz	the actress
o ator	the actor
o contador	the accountant

Parts of the Body

o braço	the arm
as costas	the back
a barriga	the belly
o corpo	the body
o rabo	the tail
o cérebro	the brain
a bochecha	the cheek
o peito	the chest
a orelha	the ear
o cotovelo	the elbow
o olho	the eye
a sobrancelha	the eyebrow
o rosto	the face
o dedo	the finger
a unha	the finger nail
os dedos da mão	the fingers
o pé	the foot
a testa	the forehead
o cabelo	the hair
a mão	the hand
a cabeça	the head
o coração	the heart
o calcanhar	the heel
a anca	the hip
o maxilar	the jaw
o joelho	the knee
a perna	the leg
o lábio	the lip
o pulmão	the lung

a boca	the mouth
a unhas	the nails
o pescoço	the neck
o nariz	the nose
o ombro	the shoulder
a pele	the skin
o estômago	the stomach
a coxa	the thigh
a garganta	the throat
o polegar	the thumb
o dedo	the toe
os dedos do pé	the toes
a língua	the tongue
o dente	the tooth
o tronco	the trunk
a cintura	the waist
o punho	the wrist
tornozelo	the ankle
o rim	the kidney
o fígado	the liver
o pulmão	the lung
a veia	the vein

The Face

a sobrancelha	the eyebrow
o bigode	the moustache
a barba	the beard
a bochecha	the cheek
o queixo	the chin
o cílio	the eyelash
a orelha	the ear
a pálpebra	the eyelid
o rosto	the face
a testa	the forehead
o cabelo	the hair

a cabeça	the head
a íris	the iris
a língua	the tongue
o lábio	the lip
a boca	the mouth
o nariz	the nose
a narina	the nostril
a pupila	the pupil

Meat

toucinho	bacon
frango assado	baked chicken
galeto	barbacued chicken
vaca	beef
mortadela	bologna
galinha	chicken
salsicha	frankfurter
frango frito	fried chicken
presunto	ham
carneiro	lamb
porco	pork
lombinho de porco	pork cutlets
coelho	rabbit
rosbife	roast beef
linguiça	sausage
bife	steak
peru	turkey
vitela	veal
veado	venison

Fish/Seafood

carpa	carp
mariscada	clam
bacalhau	cod
caranguejo	crab
arenque	herring

lagosta	lobster
cavala	mackerel
polvo	octopus
ostra	oyster
camarão	prawns
salmão	salmon
sardinha	sardines
camarão	shrimp
lula	squid
peixe-espada	swordfish
truta	trout
atum	tuna

Fruits

maçã	apple
abacate	avocado
banana	banana
cereja	cherry
coco	coconut
damasco	damask
tâmara	date
figo	fig
uva	grape
toranja	grapefruit
goiaba	guava
limão	lemon
limão galego	lime
manga	mango
melão	melon
laranja	orange
mamão	papaya
maracujá	passion fruit
pêssego	peach
pêra	pear
abacaxi	pineapple
ameixa	plum
romã	pomegranate
passa	raisin

framboesa	raspberry
morango	strawberry
tangerina	tangerine
melancia	watermelon

Vegetables

alcachofra	artichoke
aspargos	asparagus
feijão	beans
beterraba	beet
pimentão	bell pepper
brócolis	broccoli
repolho	cabbage
cenoura	carrot
couve-flor	cauliflower
salsão	celery
chuchu	chayote
milho	corn
pepino	cucumber
berinjela	egg plant
alho	garlic
vagem	green bean
couve	kale
alface	lettuce
cogumelo	mushroom
quiabo	okra
azeitona	olive
cebola	onion
ervilhas	peas
batata	potato
rabanete	radish
salada	salad
soja	soy bean
espinafre	spinach
abóbora	squash
batata doce	sweet potato
tomate	tomato

| nabo | turnip |

Grains and Dairy Products

cevada	barley
feijão	beans
manteiga	butter
queijo	cheese
creme	cream
sorvete	ice cream
margarina	margarine
leite	milk
aveia	oat
picolé	popsicle
arroz	rice
centeio	rye
trigo	wheat
nata	whipped cream
iogurte	yogurt

Table Items

tigela	bowl
xícara	cup
louça	dishes
garfo	fork
frigideira	frying pan
copo	glass
chaleira	kettle (tea)
faca	knife
guardanapo	napkin
panela	pan
pimenteira	peppershaker
jarra	pitcher
prato	plate
saleiro	saltshaker

pires	saucer
talheres	silverware
colher	spoon
toalha de mesa	tablecloth
bandeja	tray

Spices and Desserts

bolo	cake
canela	cinnamon
cacao	cocoa
biscoitos	cookies
alho	garlic
mel	honey
sorvete	ice cream
geléia	jam
gelatine	jello
ketchup	ketchup
mostarda	mustard
creme de amendoim	peanut butter
pimenta	pepper
torta	pie
pudim	pudding
sal	salt
açúcar	sugar
vinagre	vinegar

Drinks

batida de coco	coconut smoothie
batida de limão	lemon smoothie
chá preto	black tea
conhaque	brandy
cachaça	cachaça
caipirinha	caipirinha
champanhe	champagne
chocolate gelado	chocolate ice cream
coca-cola	coca-cola
coquetel	cocktail

café com leite	coffee with milk
café	coffee
pinga	pinga
gim	gin
guaraná	guarana
chocolate quente	hot chocolate
suco	juice
limonada	lemonade
licor	liquor
chá mate	mate tea
chimarrão	mate
leite	milk
água mineral	mineral water
suco de laranja	orange juice
laranjada	orange juice
suco de abacaxi	pineapple juice
quentão	quentão
vinho tinto	red wine
refresco	refreshment
rum	rum
água tônica	tonic
uísque	whiskey
vinho branco	white wine
vinho	wine

Parts of the House

a sala (de estar)	the (living) room
o apartamento	the apartment
o sótão	the attic
a varanda	the balcony
o porão	the basement
a banheira	the bathtub
o banheiro	the bathroom
a campainha	the bell
o tijolo	the brick
o armário	the cabinet / wardrobe
o carpete	the carpet
o teto	the ceiling

a chaminé	the chimney
a sala de jantar	the dining room
a porta	the door
o andar de baixo	the downstairs
a lareira	the fireplace
o chão, o piso	the floor
a garagem	the garage
a horta	the garden
o jardim	the garden
o portão	the gate
o quarto de hóspedes	the guest room
o corredor	the hall
o corrimão	the handrail
o lar	the home
a casa	the house
o interfone	the intercom
a cozinha	the kitchen
a escada	the ladder
o escritório	the office
a despensa	the pantry
a piscina	the pool
o telhado	the roof
o quarto	the room
o chuveiro	the shower
as escadas	the stairs
o degrau	the step
o vaso, a privada	the toilet
o andar de cima	the upstairs
a parede, o muro	the wall
o poço	the well
a janela	the window
o quintal	the yard

Clothing and Accessories

a mochila	the backpack
a bolsa	the bag
o cinto	the belt

o biquini	the bikini
as botas	the boots
o sutiã	the bra
o boné	the cap
a roupa	the clothing
o casaco	the coat
o vestido	the dress
os brincos	the earrings
a pasta	the folder
as luvas	the gloves
o chapéu	the hat
a jaqueta	the jacket
a calça jeans	the jeans
os jeans	the jeans
a jaqueta de couro	the leather jacket
a mini-saia	the miniskirt
o colar	the necklace
a gravata	the necktie
as malas	the packing
o pijama	the pajamas
a calcinha	the panties
as calças	the pants
a carteira	the wallet
as sandálias	the sandals
o cachecol	the scarf
a camisa	the shirt
os sapatos	the shoes
o short	the short
a bermuda	the shorts
as pantufas	the slippers
a blusa	the smock
o tênis	the sneaker
os tênis	the sneakers
as meias	the socks
o terno	the suit
o suéter	the sweater
o moletom	the sweatshirt
o maiô	the swimsuit
o anél	the ring

a saia	the skirt
o smoking	the tuxedo
a cueca	the underwear

Countries

África	Africa
Albânia	Albania
América	America
Argentina	Argentina
Ásia	Asia
Austrália	Australia
Áustria	Austria
Bélgica	Belgium
Bolívia	Bolivia
Brasil	Brazil
Bulgária	Bulgaria
Canadá	Canada
China	China
Croácia	Croatia
República Tcheca	Czech Republic
Dinamarca	Denmark
Egito	Egypt
Inglaterra	England
Europa	Europe
Finlândia	Finland
França	France
Alemanha	Germany
Grã-Bretanha	Great Britain
Grécia	Greece
Índia	India
Indonésia	Indonesia
Irlanda	Ireland
Israel	Israel
Itália	Italy
Japão	Japan
Coréia	Korea

Lituânia	Lithuania
Macedônia	Macedonia
Malta	Malta
Marrocos	Morocco
Holanda	Netherlands
Nova Zelândia	New Zealand
Noruega	Norway
Peru	Peru
Polônia	Poland
Portugal	Portugal
Romênia	Romania
Rússia	Russia
Escócia	Scotland
Senegal	Senegal
Eslováquia	Slovakia
Eslovênia	Slovenia
Espanha	Spain
Suécia	Sweden
Suíça	Switzerland
Tunísia	Tunisia
Turquia	Turkey
Ucrânia	Ukraine
Reino Unido	United Kingdom
Estados Unidos	United States
Vietnã	Vietnam
País de Gales	Wales

Nationalities

africano/africana	African
albanês/albanesa	Albanian
americano/americana	American
argentino/argentina	Argentinian
asiático/asiática	Asian
australiano/australiana	Australian
austríaco/austríaca	Austrian
belga	Belgian
boliviano/boliviana	Bolivian
brasileiro/brasileira	Brazilian

búlgaro/búlgara	Bulgarian
canadense	Canadian
chinês/chinesa	Chinese
croata	Croatian
tcheco/tcheca	Czech
dinamarquês/dinamarquesa	Danish
egípcio/egípcia	Egyptian
inglês/inglesa	English
europeu/européia	European
finlandês/finlandesa	Finnish
francês/francesa	French
alemão/alemã	German
inglês/inglesa	British
grego/grega	Greek
indiano/indiana	Indian
indonésio/indonésia	Indonesian
irlandês/irlandesa	Irish
israelense/israelita	Israeli
italiano/italiana	Italian
japonês/japonesa	Japanese
coreano/coreana	Korean
lituano/lituana	Lithuanian
macedônio/macedônia	Macedonian
maltês/maltesa	Maltese
marroquino/marroquina	Moroccan
holandês/holandesa	Dutch
neozelandês/neozelandesa	New Zealander
nogueguês/norueguesa	Norwegian
peruano/peruana	Peruvian
polonês/polonesa	Polish
português/portuguesa	Portuguese
romeno/romena	Romanian
russo/russa	Russian
escocês/escocesa	Scottish
senegalês/senegalesa	Senagalese
eslovaco/eslovaca	Slovak
eslovênio/eslovênia	Slovene
espanhol/espanhola	Spanish
sueco/sueca	Swedish

suíço/suíça	Swiss
tunísio/tunísia	Tunisian
turco/turca	Turk
ucraniano/ucraniana	Ukrainian
inglês/inglesa	English
americano/americana	American
vietnamita	Vietnamese
galês/galesa	Welsh

Sports

atletismo	athletics
beisebol	baseball
basquete	basketball
boliche	bowling
boxe	boxing
canoagem	canoeing
alpinismo	climbing
ciclismo	cycling / biking
dardos	darts
pesca	fishing
futebol americano	football
golfe	golf
hóquei	hockey
andar a cavalo	horse hiding
karatê	karate
pingue-pongue	ping pong
rúgbi	rugby
corrida	running
vela	sailing
mergulho	scuba diving
esqui	ski
paraquedismo	skydiving
sinuca - bilhar	snooker
futebol	soccer
surfe	surfing
natação	swimming
tênis	tennis
voleibol	volleyball

caminhada	walking
esqui aquático	water-skiing
luta livre	wrestling

CPSIA information can be obtained
at www.ICGtesting.com
Printed in the USA
LVHW080426190722
723834LV00015B/1116